Catching Shadows

Tying Flies for
the Toughest Fish
and Strategies
for Fishing Them

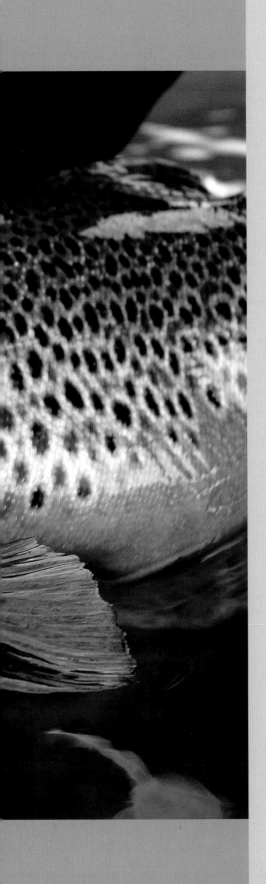

Catching Shadows

Tying Flies for
the Toughest Fish
and Strategies
for Fishing Them

RICH STROLIS

HeadWater
Books

STACKPOLE
BOOKS

Published by
STACKPOLE BOOKS
5067 Ritter Road
Mechanicsburg, PA 17055
www.stackpolebooks.com

Printed in the United States of America

10 9 8 7 6 5 4 3 2 1

First edition

Cover design by Wendy A. Reynolds
Cover image by Tommy Baranowski
Image on pages ii and iii by Justin Hansen
Photos by the author except where noted

Cataloging-in-Publication data is on file with the Library of Congress.

ISBN 978-0-8117-1329-0

This book is dedicated to my lovely wife, Megan;
to our two beautiful daughters, Tessa and Nora;
and to my Mom and Dad.

Without all of your support, I may have never pursued
my passion, and I love you all dearly because of it.

Contents

Acknowledgments

Far too many people have influenced me along the way to thank, so I apologize first if I left you out. Please realize I am grateful regardless. First, I want to thank my parents, Dale and Richard Strolis—the best a kid could ask for. Without your guidance, there is no way that I would be where I am today, and I am forever indebted to you. To my lovely wife, Megan, and our two daughters, Tessa and Nora, words cannot express my gratitude for your patience and support throughout this project and for allowing me to pursue my passion.

To my late grandmother Josephine Strolis, although you are no longer with us in body, your spirit is still close by. All those days spent together at the nearby brook chasing natives are forever ingrained in my soul. To my late great-uncle Joe, although I never fished with you, your collection of fishing equipment sparked an interest in me that continues to burn strong.

To Thomas Ames Jr., if it wasn't for you, I might never have crossed over into the business side of fly fishing. Your words of encouragement, and prodding, set me on the path to become a guide, signature fly designer, and teacher. To you I am forever indebted, and I'm thankful that our paths crossed. Hopefully, we can fish together again soon or collect some bugs like old times.

To David Goulet for your wealth of knowledge, for being a friend, and for allowing me to pester you at your shop while you were busy tying size 32 Parachutes. Oh, and thanks for sharing your coffee with me on a regular basis and making me a better fly tier and thinker; your generosity never goes unnoticed.

To my gaggle of fishing cronies from the Housy—Mike Klubek, Torrey Collins, and Steve Yoos—hopefully we can hit the water again soon like old times.

To John Miller of the Westbranch Angler, one of the best guys, photographers, and guides I know. Your contributions to the book are outstanding, and I am honored to include them.

To Don Barnes of Regal Engineering, you have been a consummate professional, and I appreciate everything that you have done for me. Your vises are second to none, and I am proud to be a part of a great American-made product; Regal vises are simply the best.

To Mark Hamnett of Partridge, for your awesome hooks and generous nature every time we cross paths.

To John Torok and Andrew Dickinson at Hatch Reels, thanks for making me a part of your team and taking care of me whenever I needed a reel for guiding or my own personal excursions. You have been beyond dependable, and you produce the best reels on the market.

To Martin Bawden of the Flymen Fishing Company, many thanks for all the support from you and your staff. Many of my creations were made possible by your innovative materials.

To Jake Chutz and Adam Trina of Montana Fly Company, and to behind the scenes good friend and MFC local rep Crosby Beane, for taking on my fly patterns and making me a signature designer in the best fly company in the world.

To George Daniel, you gave me the insight and assurance that this book was something that "had" to be done. I appreciate your words of encouragement and your expertise; hopefully we can hit some water together again soon.

To Matt Supinski, for your insight into writing and your down-to-earth and rather comical personality. You made me realize I need to take a deep breath and laugh.

To Dan and Tom Harrison of Harrison Anglers, you guys are the cowboys of the Northeast and two of the most motivated guides I have ever met. I am happy to call you guys friends and even more thankful for your support of my bugs, till the next unicorn hunt for that elusive 30-inch brown.

To Tommy Baranowski, the kid brother I never had. Keep pursuing your passion; you remind of a smaller version of myself.

To Justin Hansen, Pat Burke, and Derrick Kirkpatrick, for your awesome photographs and continued support of my patterns. Keep slinging the big flies in search of Walter. I'll keep coming up with patterns for you.

To Joshua Fine, my biggest fan and best client. You have an uncanny way of coming up with great fly names, so I appreciate the insight and help. You also need to move back up this way, so we can fish more often.

To all the personalities that I have had the pleasure of sitting next to at all the regional fly-tying shows and become friends with. Michael Schmidt (my brother from another mother), Pat Cohen, Kevin Compton, Allen Landheer, John Collins, Steve Silverio, Mike Heck, Greg Senyo, Jim Froio, Scott Hunter, and all the rest of you whom I have had the pleasure of meeting along the way, you have been inspiring.

To all the fly shops, clubs, and members who invited me into your homes to share my passion of our lovely sport, the list is long, and I thank you all for that opportunity.

To Jay Nichols, my editor, who felt my patterns were noteworthy enough to put to paper. You have made me a better writer and photographer, and I greatly appreciate your guidance.

And lastly to everyone whom I have guided, tied flies for, or met along the way. Without all of you, none of this would be possible, and I hope you glean something valuable from pages that follow.

Foreword

Hours had passed since twilight's last gleaming, but still I pressed on. In Connecticut, as in most New England states, my license could be revoked, or worse, if I were caught fishing an hour or more after sunset. I was not, however, looking for fish. As a writer and amateur fly-fishing entomologist, I was hopscotching my way up the Farmington River to capture and photograph aquatic insect samples, using a trick that I had learned from real, academically certified entomologists. They gather specimens of adult insects by reflecting ultraviolet light off a white reflector, to which many nocturnal insects are attracted. I was hunting for caddisflies.

About two miles downstream from Hogback Dam, which releases cold, nutrient-rich water to this remarkable fishery, I turned left onto a dirt road, not only to follow the river, but also to shake off an irritating pair of headlights that had been dogging me for the last mile or so. The ruse failed. The pursuer and his blinding beams remained on my heel. When I pulled sharply to the side of the road to let the driver pass, bright blue lights flashed in my mirrors.

Panic quickly gave way to amusement. Only one law enforcement officer in the entire state of Connecticut would go out of his way to follow a high-mileage SUV with bug-referencing Vermont vanity plates along a prime stretch of a fly-fishing river at an hour so close to midnight. Sure enough, when the unmarked cruiser pulled alongside and lowered its power windows, I recognized my tormentor: Rich Strolis.

I had met Rich some years before when, as the program coordinator for the Farmington River Anglers Association. He recruited me to give a presentation to the club in New Hartford, Connecticut. He also accepted the duty of entertaining me, the club's out-of-town guest speaker, by introducing me to some of the Farmington's best pools and runs.

Several things struck me about our time on the river that afternoon. First, this young man—we are decades apart in age—knew every rock, riffle, and run in the entire protected 4-mile stretch of the Farmington TMA (Trout Management Area). Second, he was entirely focused on creating an enjoyable experience for his guest. I don't think he even put his own rod together. I only fish with guides when somebody else is picking up the tab, but in Rich I recognized all of the qualities of a guide-in-the-making, and I told him so. That may not have been the best advice to give a newly married man with a full-time job as a Connecticut State Trooper, but the deed was done. Rich spent the next ten years guiding clients on the best trout waters of western Connecticut and Massachusetts.

We've since spent time together exploring several of those rivers for both fish and the bugs that they eat. The difference between then and now is that the relationship is more interdependent: I am as fascinated by the patterns and techniques that Rich has developed to imitate the insects in a trout's diet as Rich is by my studies of the insects he imitates. Like Rich, and partly under his influence, I have also embraced the joys of casting large streamers—imitations of baitfish—and hauling in correspondingly large fish.

In the years since that afternoon outing, Rich has done just about everything but sleep. He remains in law enforcement, although he logs fewer nighttime prowling hours these days and more daytime hours as an educator. He's taking a break from guiding, but only because raising two daughters takes up most of the waking hours of merely mortal men. (I know this from experience.) Somehow, Rich still finds the time to fish for all things with fins and dream up new ways to catch them. His waking dreams include some of the most innovative fly patterns you are likely to find anywhere, along with a whole new mindset about fly-pattern design.

What Rich represents is the new generation of Eastern fly fishers and fly designers. Raised in the corner of the New World that gave birth to American fly fishing, he is shaking off the decades-old shackles of tradition. Bamboo and broughams may look good on the cover of your favorite fly-fishing magazine, but they won't stand up to the rigors of foul-weather wading and precise presentation. Fur and feathers were fine in their day and may still have their place, but a surge in synthetic stuff has opened new doors for creative fly design in an era when fishing pressure has raised the bar on both imitation and presentation, and in an environment that can be unkind to the contents of your fly boxes. If you've ever selected a Pheasant Tail Nymph that you crafted so painstakingly last year, only to discover that its tail has been chewed off by some microscopic critter, you'll appreciate the longevity of synthetics. Ironically, many of the newer, manufactured materials behave more naturally in the water than their "natural" counterparts, plus they require less prep time before use and are more durable.

Rich will introduce you to an abundance of new tying techniques, tools, and materials. Read carefully, however, and you will discover that Rich is writing not just for anglers who like to tie their own flies. He is writing for fly designers as well. Just notice how he writes about a fly's "acoustic footprint" or about how it "tracks" through the water, or when he discusses "articulated" streamers or "finesse patterns." Where traditionalists are still employing the venerable "Leisenring lift" or the once-heretical "sudden inch," Rich meditates on fishing a fly with the proper cadence or using the latest Euro nymphing techniques, such as the greased coiled sighter.

In developing his twenty-first-century patterns, Rich has embraced a twentieth-century idea, a tenet of the Bauhaus design movement known as "the elegant solution" that I heard over and over from my design teacher in college back in the seventies. It's the same principle that Steve Jobs adopted for the clean, yet high-tech design of products and packaging at Apple. Rich calls it by its other name: the "less is more" philosophy. Each of his patterns comes with a story about searching for—and finding—exactly the right material and using it in exactly the right way to create exactly the right effect. The result is engineering economy, both in the number and quantity of materials and in the time required to assemble them into a finished and supremely effective fly.

By the way, Rich is no slacker when it comes to aquatic entomology. Shortly after lighting up my rear-view mirror on that dark Farmington night, he lit up a submerged branch with his bright policeman's flashlight to expose an elusive population of *Siphlonurus* mayfly nymphs—something I had not seen on that river in ten years of searching. Now, some ten years later, he is again showing something new to all of us who like to tie flies and cast them to trout.

Thomas Ames Jr.
November 2014

Introduction

My goal in this book is not only to share a variety of fly patterns that I've devised, but to give you an idea of how important tying flies can be to your growth as an angler. I hope this book inspires some of you to tie your own flies, or if you are already tying, to constantly experiment with your designs, both at the bench and on the water. Pick apart the patterns. Figure out why a fly is successful and what the triggers are, or why a certain pattern fished in a particular manner produces fish when other techniques will not. Tying flies that catch fish is one thing; knowing why they catch fish is another.

I firmly believe that fly fishermen who tie their own flies have an advantage over those who don't. Tiers can fine-tune their flies, but the angler who buys flies must rely on the patterns from a catalog or fly shop. This isn't a knock on those who don't tie their own flies, just an observation based on years of experience and the knowledge that I steadily progressed as a fly angler as a result of tying my own flies. Sound techniques, casting ability, presentation, and understanding of the species you are targeting by far surpass fly selection in importance, but all of the accomplished anglers that I have crossed paths with over the years tie their own flies.

Tying flies in succession is the cornerstone for consistency. If you tie the same fly in multiples of six to twelve, you not only strive to make each copy the same, but you'll also have logged the recipe into your memory bank for future reference.

There's nothing more satisfying than heading out on a fishing trip with a box overflowing with patterns you tied yourself. Even more rewarding is catching fish on those same flies.

One byproduct of tying your own flies is that you'll understand the steps involved in designing a solid pattern. Tying a good pattern is like building a house: you need a strong foundation before you can set the walls and roof; otherwise, it will collapse. Fly design works in the same manner: without a sound foundation and a well-thought-out design, a pattern will fail when it hits the water. Many variables come into play. One of the most important is the properties of specific materials. If you understand how a material will behave in the water, you'll be able not only to recreate popular fly patterns, but also to create something fresh. I learned the importance of understanding the limitations of materials early on and was influenced by local legend Dave Goulet, who owned a fly shop on the banks of the Farmington River in New Hartford, Connecticut. Ahead of his time in fly innovation, Dave understood the limitations of materials while also building patterns around triggers and layers of color. Dave, a commercial fly tier and designer, had an uncanny ability to simplify a particular concept or trigger for a species of fish or a particular hatch and concoct a successful, easy-to-tie pattern. I learned from him that sometimes anglers and tiers overthink things when the answer to a problem is simple.

When it comes to designing fly patterns, we're in an exciting era. Synthetic materials are evolving at an incredible rate, and we now have a huge selection of them at our disposal.

Tying your own flies is a chance to get creative, as every season my fly boxes evolve. Whether it's something entirely new or just a minor adjustment to a pattern I trust, the patterns always change based upon their effectiveness on the water.

A fully stocked streamer box with a variety of confidence patterns. It's often more beneficial to have variety in your fly box rather than dozens and dozens of the same pattern. Every season my streamer boxes change based mostly on the prevailing conditions.

Synthetics are great from a commercial tier's perspective, as you pretty much get 100-percent usable material in every package you purchase. Natural materials like feathers and furs, although hard to imitate in their properties, have varying yields of usable material per package. Both natural and synthetic materials have their place, but with diminishing supplies of some natural materials, many tiers are forced to search out alternatives for them. The flipside, however, is there's also a multitude of dyed natural materials available at a fairly reasonable price from a variety of companies. The days spent searching for that certain color of a particular fur or feather, or dyeing it yourself, are gone, as one can find a majority of these items with a few clicks of a mouse.

Today, more than ever, we have a growing community through social media and the Internet of fishermen and tiers from all over the globe, and connecting and sharing ideas is much easier than in times past. A simple email or a comment on a picture can spark interest while also further helping to develop a pattern. I've made some of my closest fishing friends initially through the Internet, only to later meet in person at some of the winter fly-fishing shows.

Throwing a bunch of pretty materials together on a hook without any thought into how they behave may work at times, but you'll find more often that this approach will fail. Good fly patterns aren't typically good by chance. They are well-thought-out designs that may have come together over time and are grounded by important ideas, traits, and concepts. Without these key ingredients, you'll have problems that may slow or stop the progress of your pattern, and you may waste quality materials in the meantime. Spending some time sketching out ideas on paper is far more beneficial and efficient than just grabbing stuff off the bench and haphazardly attaching it to a hook.

To design a solid fly pattern, you need the ability to visualize your idea in reverse. Once you have an idea of what a pattern is going to look like or how it should behave, you need to understand that the hook is your canvas and be familiar with how much space you're working with, while also maintaining the proper dimensions of whatever it is you plan to imitate. This is most important when imitating insects, as trout can be selective not just about the type of insect they choose to eat, but also about the size and color. Often, multiple species of mayflies will hatch on the same stretch of water, and at each current seam, the trout feeding on the surface can be eating entirely different insects. On highly pressured waters, if your imitation is not close in size, color, and shape to what the trout are feeding on, you may not catch anything.

This book is not just a showcase of my own creations; it is really a collection of ideas and tying concepts that I hope will bring out the creative side in you. I don't take credit as the inventor of any of them, but rather as an educator on the effectiveness and efficiency that they provide the fly tier. I have been influenced by countless people along the way, many who are recognized nationally in the industry, and some you've never heard of. I hope, after reading this book, you gain some insight into my thought process on the patterns I've come up with and why I tied them in the manner that I did. I also hope that some of the tricks that I developed over the years will help you be more efficient when you're at the vise tying flies for your next outing, so you can spend more time doing what we all enjoy: fishing. Always try to be consistent with your flies, push the envelope with materials, and continue to make your flies better until you feel that they cannot be improved. In the end, I hope that this book will inspire you, as so many people before me have inspired my own tying and fishing.

PART I
Dry Flies & Emergers

CHAPTER 1

Designing Dry Flies & Emergers

For a majority of us who started out fly fishing, the image of a trout rising to intercept an insect floating on the surface is what comes to mind whenever anyone mentions our sport. Even better are those days when we're fortunate enough to cast to those rising fish and hook up with them on a regular basis. There's nothing more rewarding than the sight of your dry fly disappearing into the ring of a trout that sipped your offering after you made that perfect cast and drag-free drift.

Dry flies and emergers can be classified in two general categories: hatch-matching patterns or general attractors. Some patterns actually can act as both at times, so the line between categories is vague. Most of the surface-oriented fishing in my region, the Northeast, swings more toward the hatch-matching side of the spectrum, so many of the flies that I tie and fish are designed specifically around a certain type of insect. That being

Fly fishing brings us to many beautiful places, regardless of the size of the body of water. Brook trout are some of the most enjoyable fish to chase, and prospecting for them with dry flies in mountain streams can be rewarding fishing.

The allure of rising trout is what drew many of us anglers to this wonderful sport. The rhythmic cadence of an elegant cast that lands softly on the water's surface is second only to that brief moment when a trout sips your fly.

said, you will also find that some of the patterns in this book are good searching patterns during periods of little to no hatch activity. For the most part, I would say that just about any successful dry-fly pattern could be considered a searching pattern from time to time, thus sliding it into the category of an attractor. But not all attractors can be hatch-specific patterns.

Most of my hatch-matching patterns were designed to fool tough fish that lazily feed in slicks, backwaters, and glides that require precise presentations. Even though these fish may be well-conditioned machines that will turn their noses at the slightest mistake in presentation, or any difference in fly size, they don't necessarily require complex patterns.

The water types where you fish your flies will play a large part in determining the materials you'll incorporate into the design of your surface patterns. Even with the advent of synthetic materials, most surface-oriented patterns still rely on natural materials. With the exception of closed-cell foam, natural feathers and furs make up the bulk of the dry-fly patterns. Some of these natural materials have natural oils built into them that shed water well and are difficult to replicate. Cul de canard (CDC) feathers, for example, have oils from the glands of a duck or goose, which naturally shed water and make for great winging material. Conversely, snowshoe rabbit fur is equally water-resistant but far more durable. Alone, these materials will suffice in situations with calmer water. Once you add turbulence to the equation, you may want to consider patterns built out of synthetics like foam, heavily hackled bodies, excessive amounts of highly buoyant materials like snowshoe rabbit fur, or a combination of these ingredients.

When it comes to designing dry flies and emergers, less is more. A plethora of complex dry-fly patterns work well, but from my experience, they don't work any better than some of the much simpler patterns that are readily available. On pressured trout streams, if the fish are keying in on emergers, then my fly will have three main ingredients: shuck, body, and wing.

If they're keying in on adults, then the fly should have a tail, body, and wing. If the fish are feeding on spent adults or spinners, then the fly should have a tail, body, and spent wing. By keeping it simple, you not only give the fish less to look at on the water, you also don't feel so bad when you break one of your flies off in the bushes behind you or in the mouth of a trout. Often, when you tie dry flies with multiple materials and steps, you will also alter the overall dimensions of the fly pattern, which can quickly equate to a long day casting but not catching.

Pay attention to the fine details. Three characteristics are of utmost importance in any dry-fly or emerger pattern: size, color, and shape. From my experience, when fishing with surface patterns over educated trout, these three attributes come into play more so than in any other type of fly fishing. During periods of selective feeding, trout that are keyed in on specific insects will simply turn down imitations that aren't close to the real thing. Sometimes, you may only need to match one of the three criteria, as there are varying levels of selectivity, while at other times on pressured waters, your imitation will get snubbed unless all three attributes match the naturals precisely. You'll often encounter fishing situations where a single pattern with the size, color, and shape of the naturals outperforms any other pattern.

You can, however, think of these three attributes loosely. You don't have to spend countless hours at the vise concocting super-realistic imitations of all of your favorite hatches each season. If you are so inclined, then by all means do so, but in the end, if you follow these three attributes, you should have a selection of dry flies that will work in a wide variety of situations.

Of the three main attributes of flies, I do, however, believe that there is a hierarchy in regard to their importance. First, I will try to match the size of the naturals as best I can. Usually, if I can present a fly that is close to the shape and size of the naturals,

I like to keep things simple, so multi-species patterns are my bread-and-butter dry flies every season. Once I find a fly that works well, I like to tie versions of it in the predominant colors that I encounter in a season.

Prospecting with dry-fly patterns can be a viable option even when there's little to no hatch activity. This trick isn't region-specific; it will work just about anywhere there is moving water. MIKE SCHMIDT

approximately half of the time this will suffice even if the color of the fly isn't an exact match. If, however, I choose a fly that's close in size to the naturals but not the same color and it is continually refused, then I regroup and find a fly that will match the natural in both size and color. This may require a little streamside capturing of insects and close inspection of the naturals. You can keep a small aquarium net in your vest or pack for times like these, but it isn't necessary. I have found that my hands will often suffice, and I can easily scoop up a bug or two from the surface film. I have also used my baseball cap to accomplish the task, and on hot summer days, this serves a dual purpose as a cooling system once I place it back on my head.

The size of your imitation needs to be relatively close, and the proportions should be as well. Caddisflies, for example, on average have a body that is two-thirds the length of their wing, and selective trout will notice if your wings and bodies are not in sync. Some mayflies have short, stout bodies with above-average-length wings, while others are longer and more slender. Taking the time to inspect what hatches on your waters will give you a better idea of how to recreate those flies and how to up your game on the water.

Lastly, color, although important, is less significant than size and shape. In fact, I have had instances where using a fly that was actually a shade different in color than the naturals worked better than an exact match. This has typically been the case during periods of heavy emergence. Some of our local Sulphur hatches can be prolific, with bugs blanketing the

water's surface every couple of inches. This can be maddening, especially if the trout are feeding with reckless abandon and you can't seem to distinguish your fly from the rest.

Every fish you encounter has a distinct attitude, and if you pay close attention, you will quickly learn if they are vulnerable to your method of angling. Case in point, I primarily fish emergers during mayfly emergences. In my experience, trout will key in on the most vulnerable stage of an emergence, as the insects in that particular stage are rendered helpless. My mayfly selections lean heavily on emerger patterns, but I do have some adult patterns close by if need be. For stoneflies, on the other hand, I tend to fish more adult patterns, and I tend to fish an even mix of adults and emergers for both midges and caddis. Experience has shown me that because many mayfly species take more time to metamorphose from nymph to adult, they tend to get eaten predominantly during that transitional phase. Some specific instances like spinner falls, for example, are such hit-or-miss events for the casual angler—even for the full-time angler—that I don't typically carry a large assortment of these types of patterns. My spinners are usually confined to a smaller box with a wide variety of sizes. As I said earlier, I like to keep it simple, and I've adopted this less-is-more mentality with my fly selections too. Each season I typically carry a couple of fly boxes of dry flies that are usually one or two patterns tied in a variety of colors and sizes, as I have that much faith in my flies' design and in my ability to present these flies to the fish.

CHAPTER 2

R-F Caddis

Caddis hatches can be some of the most exciting hatches for a fly fisherman. They are typically prolific and often make trout feed in a frenzied manner. Every season I have encounters with caddis that border on grotesque, due to the clouds of thousands of these insects as they swarm the air around the waters I'm fishing. Some of these hatches are so heavy that when driving home I have to use my windshield wipers just to clear their carnage from my windows as they pepper my car, swarming en masse to their temporary homes.

If you're in the right place at the right time when one of these hatches erupts, it can be nonstop fast action, and the strikes can be nothing short of vicious. As long as your fly is remotely close in color and size, you will typically be successful unless the trout

Many dry-fly patterns are imitations of one specific type of insect. The R-F Caddis is not only a good imitation of a caddisfly, it can also be used as a mayfly emerger in a pinch.

are keying in on the pupal forms below the surface. Often, the trout will get up into the heads of the pools, riffles and runs and slash at the surface, eating the adults and pupae before they fly away. From the time they emerge from their pupal shucks and reach the surface, they can easily fly away within seconds, and trout take notice. Many times during a caddisfly emergence I've witnessed large fish coming completely out of the water as they chased an emerging caddis, or seen the flanks of many brown trout in a shallow riffle as they gorged on emerging pupae.

When trout aren't in those types of waters feeding haphazardly on caddis adults, or when they're more selective, refusing your high-riding, heavily hackled patterns, you must have some alternatives in your box that will get the job done. Low, flush-riding patterns that sit in the film can be game changers. You can easily clip the hackles flat on the bottom of any of those aforementioned patterns, and although they will take fish at times, you'll quickly learn that a hackle-less pattern is key.

In my formative years, I, like many, fell in love with just about every dry fly using a wing of CDC feathers. They were light, cast well, floated high, and exuded a feeling of realism that no other winging material could provide. The long fibers of the CDC feather could not only be used for wings, but any errant fibers in the head area of the fly pattern could also be used to represent legs. For the most part, CDC feathers are pretty durable unless they are repeatedly raked through the jaws of toothy trout. Once you get a little fish slime on the feather, it takes a lot of brushing, drying, and working of powdered floatant into the feathers to get them back to their original state. CDC, although rich in movement and lifelike characteristics, can be troublesome once it gets in the mouth of a fish. Repeated teasing and drying will help in bringing the fly back to a fishable state, but often results in a fly that will not float for long. I used to deal with this and accept the limitations of CDC feathers because of their effectiveness. To offset the trouble of constantly having to dry the wings after every fish, I would tie

Caddisflies are easy insects to represent in fly patterns. Patterns only need to replicate a down wing over a slightly shorter body, making them great patterns for tiers of all experience levels.
JOHN MILLER

several of every color combination I used so that I could cycle through them periodically rather than spend more time brushing powdered floatant into their wings. This way, once the fly was well soaked with fish slime, I could just clip it off, set it on a drying patch, and tie on another until it, too, was in the same condition. Although this worked, it wasn't the greatest option, and it soon had me wondering if I could find something different that would work as well as CDC.

Over the years, I really grew fond of the X-Caddis pattern and fished it regularly with good success. The pattern itself is nothing more than an Elk Hair Caddis with the addition of a trailing shuck and the omission of a hackled body. This design gives the angler a pattern that rides flush in the film with the illusion that the bug has just sprung its pupal shuck and is in that short transitional phase before it flies away and sheds the shuck. During this key period of time, the insect is most vulnerable to trout. With the omission of a hackled body, the X-Caddis is similar in nature to the CDC caddis patterns that ride flush in the film, with a wing that sheds water much easier.

While the X-Caddis is effective, it's important to have options, especially for fish that have grown increasingly wary of whatever floats over their heads during a hatch. If the waters you fish are popular, it won't take too long for a trout to become selective as they soon learn that anything floating overhead may lead to a hook in the jaw. It's not because the fish have gotten smarter; it's just that they have been conditioned to associating a painful outcome with anything but a flawless imitation of the natural. Years of fishing a pressured tailwater have taught me that having alternative patterns is the key to catching fish on tough days. I like to have a good selection of confidence patterns on hand, but I leave a row or two in my box of change-up patterns for when the trout get moody.

A caddisfly adult and flies designed around them are elementary—a tent-winged pattern with some sort of body construction that is typically two-thirds to half the length of the wing. My first efforts to try and create something different were disasters. Early attempts with synthetic materials for wings

Photo of the underside and side profile of the R-F Caddis. Often, less complex patterns like the R-F Caddis that match the body, shuck, and wing of the naturals are all you need to fool fish.

looked good but didn't float well. I had the same result with natural materials, too, and gave up my ideas.

One day, before a guide trip, I figured out something by accident that had been staring me in the face the entire time. I was spinning up a pile of nymphs and mayfly emergers and figured that I had better have some caddis, as the day prior I had seen tan-bodied and green-bodied caddis hatching. As I fumbled through my materials, I found that I was out of elk hair and had no suitable deer hair. I had been using snowshoe rabbits' feet for the emergers that I was tying, and though they were picked clean of the prime fibers in the heel of the foot (they float the highest and compress the easiest under tension), I thought about substituting the snowshoe as a wing material.

Though I had always avoided using the stiffer fibers around the toes, I decided to give this part of the snowshoe rabbit a try. It had plenty of curve and crinkle and would trap air, making it buoyant. To keep the fly relatively easy, and because I preferred my caddis with some sort of shuck, I started to tie them with a short shuck of Rust Orangutan Ice Fur, a dubbed body, and then a wing of rabbit.

Rust Orangutan Ice Fur is my material of choice for emerger patterns. The color of the material is a close match to what most nymphal shucks look like, with the perfect amount of translucency and flex to imitate the natural.

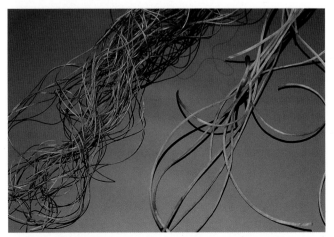

Daddy Long Legs is a much finer diameter synthetic than its big brother Life Flex or Spanflex and is the perfect material for adding legs to smaller patterns.

I tied some with tan bodies and wings, and a handful with apple green bodies and light dun wings for the day in sizes 14 to 18 just to make sure my bases were covered. I used the hair from the heel of the foot on the smaller imitations, and on the larger imitations, I used the longer, coarser hair located by the toes. I decided to fish the two for the week with clients and see if there was truly any difference in effectiveness.

The first couple of days on the water that week we saw sporadic, sometimes heavy caddis activity, with the best surface feeding later that week. My clients were my guinea pigs when I wasn't able to fish on my own, and I quickly learned some interesting things about these caddis variations. First, the imitations tied with the coarser fibers from the toe area of the rabbit's foot floated as well as those with the heel fibers. Like all snowshoe rabbit patterns, they shed water easily and were dried with floatant after several fish—back in the water quickly to fool another trout. In time, I found that I could use virtually all of the fur from the rabbit's foot.

Because of my fondness for snowshoe rabbit fur, I had acquired dozens of feet in a variety of colors for use in winging dry flies. In time, I converted all of my favorite caddis imitations to snowshoe wings and fished them regularly with clients and on my own. Because the longer toe fibers do not compress easily, it's crucial to use only a small amount of fiber in the larger versions of the R-F Caddis; otherwise, they will be overdressed. Also, if you do not build a good thread base under them, they will roll around the hook shank.

To add lifelike characteristics to the fly, I later introduced Daddy Long Legs into the pattern, tying them in a swept back manner consistent with the naturals. Over time, I have found that on finicky trout, those legs can be the difference. The Daddy Long Legs respond well with a little twitch of the fly as it rides in the slower surfaces, or while floating drag-free in water with some current. The legs will undulate and behave similarly to the legs on a natural insect, giving some added realism.

Fishing

Like many other dry-fly patterns, the R-F Caddis excels when fished dead-drift and drag-free on the surface of the water. The key to success is presenting the fly to surface-feeding fish so it not only lands softly on the water but also drifts freely in the current like a natural insect. Imparting an occasional twitch or short movement to the fly will sometimes result in a vicious strike. Many caddis will skate or skitter across the surface of the water, and trout will often give chase.

Like most surface-oriented situations, casting your fly above your target so that the fly floats into the trout's window of view is important. The currents between you and the rising fish will dictate just how much you have to lead the fly to the fish. More often than not, a fly cast a few feet above the rising trout's position is adequate, but sometimes more or less may work better.

Although it's usually a good idea to fish dry-fly patterns that closely mirror the emerging bugs, I have found that caddis patterns during the season can be fantastic searching patterns fished blind when there is little to no insect activity. Trout can be opportunistic feeders and are not always selective. Most caddis inhabit and emerge from fast-water environs, and if an opportunistic trout happens to see something that resembles a familiar food, it will often readily eat it. Fishing an R-F Caddis pattern through a particular stretch of water, targeting every likely spot that a fish may hold, is a great technique once trout season is underway. When prospecting, I make sure to concentrate my efforts in areas where trout will have little time to react by typically focusing on the moderate to faster paced water with minimal to moderate depth such as pockets, riffle heads, current seams, and plunge pools. I usually try to tackle them from a direct downstream position when my surroundings allow, but if that isn't feasible, I'll inspect the area that I want to fish first and then decide what position will allow me to present the fly drag-free.

Caddis patterns are not only great on medium to larger bodies of moving water, but also on smaller streams and creeks filled with wild trout. My small stream fly selections have always been heavy on caddis patterns, and I now use R-F Caddis patterns exclusively as my go-to caddis surface pattern.

You're probably thinking that this contradicts my earlier statement about having variety in your fly box, and you are correct. But the versatility and durability of this pattern is what has made it such a confidence fly for me.

The R-F Caddis is also fantastic in a dry-and-dropper rig, especially when fishing a lightly weighted dropper. Most dry-and-dropper rigs that I fish throughout the season are built out of small to medium dry flies with small to medium droppers. Whenever I fish this way, I prefer dry flies that resemble the insects currently available to the trout. Because I am often fishing the current seams or heads of shallow moderate to faster paced types of water, the droppers are typically shorter, usually not more than 18 to 20 inches from the R-F Caddis. Being a bit shorter, they tend to cast much easier, making for an enjoyable outing. Dry-and-dropper rigs give the fish choices; if you find that the trout are focusing solely on the surface fare as opposed to the nymphs, you might want to clip off the dropper and fish with nothing but a dry fly. When fishing new water, I often start off with a dry-and-dropper rig and then continually fine-tune the rig throughout the day.

Low-light conditions, usually in the morning or later in the day at sunset, can be great times to experience caddis hatches. Some of my most memorable experiences fishing caddis imitations have come during these times of solace.

Sometimes gently pulling the fly under the surface and allowing it to resurface can be deadly. I experimented with this tactic one day on the Housatonic River during a heavy caddis emergence with several fish breaking the surface. When I set foot into the river that morning, I saw a prolific hatch of tan caddis that seemed to have every trout and smallmouth bass in the river feeding on the surface. After about forty-five minutes of repeated drifts, tippet changes, fly changes, and additions and subtractions of droppers of various sizes and tippet lengths, I had nothing to show for it, so I sat down and regrouped. While doing so, my fly was sitting on the surface in the current several feet from the shoreline. As my fly swung across the surface and came tight, it dipped below the surface for a few seconds. As I let a little line out to lengthen my cast before pulling in my offering, my fly popped up to the surface and was immediately met with a vicious strike. I didn't land that fish, as whatever it was left with my fly in its mouth after that vicious take, but the light bulb went off in my head. These fish were eating the thousands of caddis just as they broke the surface. I took a look at the water for a few minutes and noticed that the fish were eating many of the caddis right after they broke the surface. This was a familiar tactic, as I often used this same method while fishing emerger patterns during a hatch of *Epeorus vitreus*, a larger species of Sulphur that emerges underwater and then rises through the water column as an adult.

I quickly clipped off my 6X tippet, replacing it with some 4X tippet, and added a fresh tan R-F Caddis tied on with a loop knot for additional movement. Before getting the fly wet, I dipped it into my container of Easy Dry and shook it up for a few seconds to make sure it was heavily doused in floatant. I quickly positioned myself across and upstream from a good pod of slashing fish and worked my fly by casting well above the target and waiting for my fly to get a couple of feet above where the fish were feeding before I pulled it under. After the first or second cast, I had a jolting take as the line straightened and the fish ran downstream. The bulk of the fish that day ate the fly right as it popped through the meniscus, and they did so hastily every time. After every fish or when the fly got too wet, I would shake it up in some Loon Blue Ribbon or brush some Frog's Fanny floatant into the wing and body, and it would be ready to fish within a few seconds. To this day, I never leave home without a few of these caddis imitations, and several of them have lasted multiple outings and dozens of fish.

Variations

By varying the color and size, you can imitate any of the caddis that you'll encounter. My favorite hook to tie this pattern on is a Partridge Patriot Ideal Dry, which is a black, nickel–finished, down-eye, dry-fly hook. If you can't get these exact models of hooks, any straight 1X or 2X long standard dry-fly hook will suffice. I prefer the Partridge hook, mostly because it is barbless and has a long, fine, needle-sharp beak.

In a pinch, I have used this pattern for not only a caddis but for small to medium stoneflies and also as a mayfly emerger as well. Typically I carry a few R-F Caddis in my fly box in shades

Even large browns can't resist a well-placed caddis pattern when caddis are actively hatching.

of brown and olive, and both have served well for mayfly patterns in these colors. I have used several different types of dubbing over the years for these flies, and overall my favorite dubbing has been Hareline Hare'e Ice Dub, or Jack Mickievicz's Poly & Antron Caddis Blends. This particular dubbing is soft, has great translucency, and is very lifelike. Both the Ice Dub and the Poly & Antron Caddis Blends come in all of the applicable caddis colors and are wonderful dubbings to work with for flies of all sizes, which is important because caddis come in many sizes, some small.

TAN R-F CADDIS

Hook: #10-18 Partridge Ideal Dry or Tiemco 100
Thread: Tan 140-denier Ultra Thread
Shuck: Rust Orangutan Ice Fur
Body: Tan Hareline Hare'e Ice Dub
Legs: Brown Hareline Daddy Long Legs
Wing: Tan snowshoe rabbit fur

Note: For flies smaller than a size 14, use 70-denier Ultra Thread.

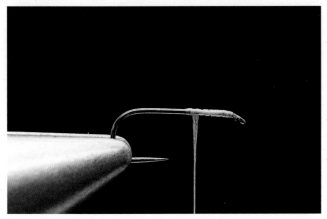

1. Attach the tying thread to the hook one half the eye's length behind the eye of the hook, and continue to a point just shy of the midpoint of the hook.

2. Grab a small hank of Ice Fur and secure it to the top of the hook shank with a few loose wraps of thread. Once you make a few turns of thread around the material, continue wrapping the thread to the end of the hook shank where the bend begins.

3. Dub a slightly tapered noodle of Hare'e Ice Dub to a point about one eye's length behind the eye. As you wrap the dubbing noodle forward toward the eye of the hook, you can preen the fibers rearward with the thumb and forefinger of your opposite hand to help build the taper.

4. Cut a section of snowshoe rabbit hair from a snowshoe rabbit foot, comb out the underfur, and secure it to the top of the hook shank with six to eight increasingly tight turns of thread. Be sure to keep pressure on the bundle on the downward turns. A drop of superglue on the thread wraps prior to securing the wing is often beneficial.

5. Cut a pair of Daddy Long Legs, and tie them in on either side of the hook shank.

6. Dub a thin noodle of Hare'e Ice Dub to the thread, and cover the thread wraps, starting from the front, then working backward toward the base of the wing. Be sure not to trim off the rabbit fur wing facing forward over the eye of the hook.

8. Trim the Daddy Long Legs so that they end at a point just past the rear of the body of the fly.

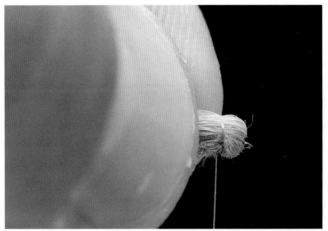

9. Underside view of the finished fly.

7. Pull the portion of the snowshoe rabbit hair that is over the eye rearward over the wing and take a few turns of thread over the bundle. Complete the fly with a four-turn whip-finish and cement the thread.

OLIVE R-F CADDIS

Hook:	#10-18 Partridge Ideal Dry or Tiemco 100
Thread:	Light olive 8/0 Uni-Thread
Shuck:	Rust Orangutan Ice Fur
Body:	Olive Hareline Hare'e Ice Dub
Legs:	Brown Hareline Daddy Long Legs
Wing:	Tan snowshoe rabbit fur

BROWN R-F CADDIS

Hook:	#10-18 Partridge Ideal Dry Tiemco 100
Thread:	Dark brown 140-denier Ultra Thread
Shuck:	Rust Orangutan Ice Fur
Body:	Olive brown Hareline Hare'e Ice Dub
Legs:	Brown Hareline Daddy Long Legs
Wing:	Rusty brown snowshoe rabbit fur

Note: For flies smaller than a size 14, use 70-denier Ultra Thread.

BLACK R-F CADDIS

Hook:	#10-18 Partridge Ideal Dry or Tiemco 100
Thread:	Black 140-denier Ultra Thread
Shuck:	Rust Orangutan Ice Fur
Body:	Black Hareline Hare'e Ice Dub
Legs:	Black Hareline Daddy Long Legs
Wing:	Black snowshoe rabbit fur

Note: For flies smaller than a size 14, use 70-denier Ultra Thread.

GREEN R-F CADDIS

Hook:	#10-18 Partridge Ideal Dry or Tiemco 100
Thread:	Olive green 140-denier Ultra Thread
Shuck:	Rust Orangutan Ice Fur
Body:	Caddis green Hareline Hare'e Ice Dub
Legs:	Brown Hareline Daddy Long Legs
Wing:	Medium dun colored snowshoe rabbit fur

Note: For flies smaller than a size 14, use 70-denier Ultra Thread.

CHAPTER 3

Dust Bunny Winter Stone

For years, I spent many cold winters trying to devise a simple, proportionate surface pattern for the little brown stoneflies and black stoneflies that hatched prolifically in the Northeast. I started out on this project with trepidation, as many of the local dry-fly experts all had varying opinions on the importance of these little bugs. Some thought they were eaten on rare occasion by chance and were not regular trout food. Others felt that they were definitely a viable option and spent a lot of time trying to mimic these little insects when they emerged. I fell somewhere in between the two extremes. I couldn't ascertain if these little insects were eaten or ignored because they hatched simultaneously with midges and Winter Caddis.

Due to the pattern's smaller size, it lands lightly on the water and rides in the surface film, much like the natural.

For years, I thought that trout were less concerned with the adults, focusing their efforts on the nymphal phase. I assumed this because the water temperatures during that particular time of the year were usually at their lowest, and as a result, trout tend to expend the least amount of energy when feeding. A trout's metabolism will be much slower in winter, so their daily nutrient requirements will be much less than in the warmer months of the year. This was my own thought related to several experiences where hundreds—if not thousands—of these tiny insects were on the surface of the water, without even a single rising trout.

I also found from years of experience that nymphs take an extended amount of time leaving the streambed on their way to emergence. I believe this is due largely to the colder water tem-

Adult Winter Stoneflies have distinctive proportions. Their bodies are thin and segmented with a pronounced pair of tented wings that extend past the body. JOHN MILLER

Smaller species of stoneflies can come in a range of colors including brown, yellow, chartreuse, or black like the insect in this picture. It often pays to have a few Dust Bunny Stones in your fly box in that variety of colors, as anyone them can hatch throughout various times of the year. JOHN MILLER

peratures when they emerge. On many occasions, I've witnessed the side-to-side wiggling action of thousands of the nymphs as they slowly ascended through the water column. I initially thought that trout just had no interest in the adults because of the reasons illustrated above. After a couple of milder winters, my thoughts began to change, as I experienced a higher frequency of rising fish to the adults. These numbers were by no means high, but they were steady enough to be noteworthy, with higher water temperatures and milder weather being the key factors that enhanced surface feeding activity to these insects.

Sporadic success with a variety of patterns over time left me with mixed feelings about whether I should delve into concocting a pattern to imitate these insects. The overall problem, more so with the tiny black specimens, was their diminutive size. The size of the naturals was close to, if not smaller than, the wire of most hooks. A dubbed body would be overdressed and too big. Many of the patterns that I had used shared a common theme: they worked on occasion but with no consistency.

Some of my earliest successes came from using simplistic flies. Elk Hair Caddis patterns with finely dubbed or thread bodies seemed to work well, but not as consistently as I'd hoped. Their durability was suspect, as they wouldn't hold up well unless I coated them with a generous layer of head cement. What troubled me more was the lack of segmentation in the body of the fly pattern. Stoneflies have pronounced, segmented bodies, and I believe that to accurately represent them your fly pattern should also have some segmentation.

Segmentation is easily accomplished on most fly patterns, but when you run into flies that are as small as the tiny black winter stoneflies, it can be problematic. To keep material bulk to a minimum, I came up with a couple of ideas. I could still build a body entirely out of thread, and use an alternative colored section of tying thread as the rib material in the body, but the end result resembled a midge more than a stonefly. My second choice was closer to what I had envisioned, and I quickly adopted a simple wrapped quill body because it was easy to work with, had fantastic segmentation, and required few thread wraps to secure to the hook shank. The key was to use a quill that would lie flat to the hook and was relatively small. My first attempts at this pattern used regular dyed stripped quills. They aren't the greatest materials to work with, as they require a great deal of prep work before you can use them. Before tying with them, you need to soak them in water half an hour to make them pliable enough to tie with. I have not found a synthetic substitute that does a better job than a properly prepared natural quill.

The next step was to lock down the winging material for this pattern, and I needed it to stay in line with my idea of devising a finesse pattern that was light, delicate, and durable. Although it is not my winging material of choice, CDC seemed like the best option for this fly. I decided that I would use only the fibers of the CDC feather, eliminating the stiff and cumbersome quill section of each feather. This may seem like a daunting task, but Marc Petitjean's Magic Tool made doing this a snap.

The Magic Tool is an ingenious device that is nothing more than a series of small tables and spring-released clamps for removing unwanted parts like a quill, for instance, while maintaining wanted material in a neat and orderly fashion. By laying your CDC feathers on top of one of the various sized tables, and then pushing them down through the center crevasse, all of the wanted fibers from the feather should stand up in a vertical position. You then take a clamp and grab those fibers from the table. After grabbing the fibers in the clamp, the quills from the feathers will be neatly in line and parallel with the face of the clamp, making it easy to clip them away while the clamp holds all the fibers neatly in alignment. Once you trim the quills away, the clamp holds the CDC fibers in place so that they can easily be added to a dubbing loop or split thread to make a dubbing brush. At this point, I wanted to add more movement and realism into the pattern, so a pair of X-tied Micro Rubber Legs much like the R-F Caddis was the trick.

Overall, this is a simple pattern that, with some planning, can be tied fairly quickly. In time I made a substitution in body material that proved to be beneficial. Once I learned about Polish Quills, pliable peacock quills that come in a variety of dyed colors, this pattern really came into its own. The Polish Quills were much more pliable than the quills that I had been using, required little to no prep work when tying with them, and they had a much nicer taper as well. If I ran into a quill that was brittle, a little vegetable oil worked into the quill would soften it up and make it useable again—a trick I learned from good friend Kevin Compton. With the introduction of blue light and UV curing resins, I substituted the head cement with a thin layer of Clear Cure Goo Hydro and the bodies of my Dust Bunny Stones were bombproof.

When tying in succession, prep work is everything. Not only do I set out piles of wings, quills, legs, and foam, but I try to arrange them in a manner that makes sense, strategically placing these materials in the order that they are tied in to cut down on wasted time. From left to right I arrange the materials in stacks: quills, CDC, legs, and foam. This way I can methodically tie several flies in succession without having to locate my next piece of the recipe. The time it takes to set up these piles of material is well worth the effort, and something I do whenever I am tying patterns in quantity.

Fishing

Due to this particular pattern's daintiness, I typically fish this fly by itself, like any other dry fly. If I'm fishing during a hatch of the much smaller, black-colored stones, even with a bright sighter of foam, they can be difficult to locate on the surface of the water, especially under low-light conditions. What I typically do under those circumstances is fish the Dust Bunny behind a larger, more visible dry fly. By doing so, I can track my drifts and get a better idea of where my fly is in the water. When a fish dimples behind the much more visible dry fly, I will set the hook, as more often than not, it has eaten the smaller Dust Bunny.

When fishing this way, a shorter section of tippet between the flies will make them easier to track with less of a chance of tangling on the cast. Minimizing drag can be problematic as well, so I recommend keeping the dropper tippet short and step-

Several size 16 Dust Bunny Winter Stones will easily fit on the face of a quarter. The foam cylinder indicator makes these tiny flies visible from great distances and also aids in the pattern's ability to float high.

ping the tippet down a size. In other words, if you are fishing 5X to the larger fly, step it down to 6X to the smaller dropper. This is a trick I use when the light is low or when fish are keying in on spinners.

I wouldn't recommend using this pattern in choppy water, as it will often get trapped in the water and sink. Due to the flush design, this fly thrives in transitional zones and slack water settings. If you find that the fish are feeding on smaller stoneflies in the faster water, fish a heavily hackled high-riding pattern instead, or simply fish a Dust Bunny Stone with more CDC in the wing.

Whenever I'm presented with feeding fish in current seams, transitions zones, or slack water settings, I have found that my positioning in relation to the fish is crucial in getting a take. On waters with strong populations of wild or wary trout, I'm most successful when I make my presentations at a downstream angle. Usually, the fish see my fly first and not my leader or fly line, and if I make that first cast count and manage to present the fly in a drag-free manner, I will more often get a take.

George Harvey's slack leader and downstream presentation are methods that I adopted specifically for situations like these, and they have made the difference for tough fish. From this angle, it's important to wait before you set the hook when a trout eats your fly. I typically will count in my head "one one-thousand" and lift; otherwise if you strike too soon, you will often pull the fly clean out of the trout's mouth before it can close its jaws on the fly.

I later adapted the pattern for Little Yellow Sallies and fished it successfully not only on the Farmington, but also on the Beaverhead in Montana, where my wife and I were greeted with a prolific hatch of them on a short family vacation. To this day, I leave room in my dry-fly boxes for a few of these bugs in a variety of colors just in case I run into trout eating smaller stoneflies.

Variations

Due to the simplicity in the design of this pattern, and because it was designed to imitate a very specific insect, this pattern doesn't have many variations. For the most part, the variations are centered around the different colors of smaller stoneflies that you may encounter on your favorite trout streams ranging in sizes from 12 to 20. My favorite color schemes are listed at the end of the chapter. As I stated earlier, if you want a bushier, higher-floating variation, then you can use more CDC feathers in the construction of the wing, or in a pinch, you could also use snowshoe rabbit hair. The only caveat with snowshoe rabbit is that you might not be able to find all the colors you need to replicate the wings of the naturals on your local streams. If you're willing to spend some time dyeing them yourself, this shouldn't be an issue. Bear in mind, they don't always have to be exact: the yellow version can work with a natural tan or light dun-colored wing for instance, as the wings of the naturals will vary depending on a wide variety of factors like time of emergence and location.

BROWN DUST BUNNY WINTER STONE

Hook:	#12-20 Partridge Ideal Dry or Tiemco 100
Thread:	Rusty brown 70- or 140-denier Ultra Thread
Body:	Brown Polish Quill
Wing:	Golden brown CDC
Legs:	Brown Hareline Daddy Long Legs
Indicator:	Yellow foam cylinder ($^1/_{16}$")

Note: Use the Tiemco 5212 for longer versions.

1. Attach the tying thread directly behind the hook eye, and work your way to the midpoint of the shank. Attach a Polish Quill by the tip and continue wrapping your thread down to the point where the bend starts and then back toward the front to a position about $^1/_4$ the length of the shank behind the eye.

2. Wrap the Polish Quill in close slightly overlapping consecutive wraps until you reach your hanging thread. Wrap over the Polish Quill three turns in front and back then half hitch your thread and clip the excess quill section.

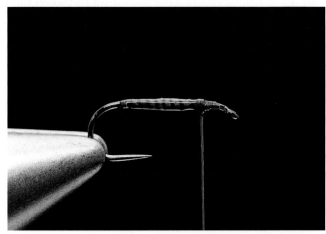

3. Coat the quill in a thin layer of head cement or Clear Cure Goo Hydro resin and cure with the UV torch. This helps build durability into the fly. If you were to leave the quill without a top coat, it would break after a few fish.

4. Select a pair of CDC feathers and preen the fibers rearward.

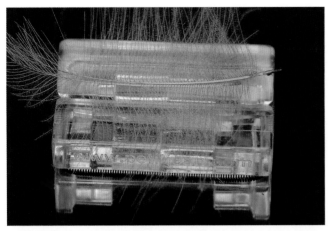

5. Lay the two CDC feathers on top of one another on the top of a Petitjean Magic Tool table. Be sure the stems curve in the same direction or else you will fight the feathers.

6. Pull the two feathers into the table using a small section of wire.

7. Remove the two married feathers from the table using the Petitjean Clamp, and then trim away the stems. Once you remove the stems, either affix the tips in a dubbing loop or split the thread and sandwich the fibers between and spin the thread locking the fibers into a rope.

8. Wrap the CDC rope forward on the hook while preening the fibers up and rearward on the hook. Make your last wrap approximately a hook eye's distance back from the eye.

9. Cut a pair of Daddy Long Legs, and tie them in on top of the hook with two thread turns. Pull one to the near side and the other to the far side and make six more turns of thread to splay the legs like an X. When tying in bulk, be sure to cut several sections to length ahead of time.

10. Make two loose thread wraps over the center of a bright yellow cylinder on top of the wing. After a half hitch, complete a four-turn whip-finish and cement the thread wraps and clip the thread. Trim the foam cylinder so that it is short near the eye.

11. Invert the fly in your vise and trim the legs to the desired length. I personally like them a bit longer than most, as you get more movement out of them.

BLACK DUST BUNNY WINTER STONE

Hook:	#12-20 Partridge Ideal Dry or Tiemco 100
Thread:	Black 70- or 140-denier Ultra Thread
Body:	Natural Polish Quill
Wing:	Black CDC
Legs:	Black Hareline Daddy Long Legs
Indicator:	Yellow foam cylinder ($1/16$")

12. Trim the CDC on the underside of the fly with a pair of fine-tipped scissors to expose the body of the fly.

GOLDEN DUST BUNNY WINTER STONE

Hook:	#12-20 Partridge Ideal Dry or Tiemco 100
Thread:	Yellow 70- or 140-denier Ultra Thread
Body:	Yellow Polish Quill
Wing:	Golden brown CDC
Legs:	Brown Hareline Daddy Long Legs
Indicator:	Chartreuse foam cylinder ($1/16$")

CHAPTER 4

Shucked Up Emerger

On my home water, the Farmington, there are what I call gangs of fishermen, many of whom are retired older fellas who gather daily on the banks of the river. Some of these anglers seem to know every trout in a given stretch of water, as they will often have names for these fish after catching them multiple times in a season. The result is heavily pressured fish that require more sophisticated flies and precise presentations.

I quickly learned what kind of presentations and types of flies will get the most attention. Because many of the regularly surface-oriented feeders preferred feeding lanes in the slicks and softer water a majority of the time, I needed to fish patterns with footprints that closely matched the naturals. My fly had to resemble what the trout were seeing, or it would be a long, frustrating day on the water. Emergers or flush-riding adult imitations were the key in those scenarios. Many of the famous high-riding and heavily hackled Catskill-style dry flies

By merely changing the thread color of the Shucked Up Emerger, dubbing color and snowshoe rabbit color, you can easily imitate virtually any mayfly that you encounter.

that I fished on the roiled waters of my youth were no match to these kinds of patterns in these situations, and they would often go untouched.

When I was younger, I would trim the hackles flat on the underside of these classic patterns with inconsistent success. Simplicity was often the answer: many patterns like Compara-duns, Snowshoe Emergers, CDC Emergers, and Haystacks would consistently yield more fish than those classic patterns. I wanted something with my own personal flare, a little different than the rest, but with some influence from those patterns listed above. Selecting favorable attributes from your favorite patterns and molding them into a fly you can call your own is very rewarding. Constantly having something just a shade different from what everyone else is casting can also be the difference. All fly fishermen strive to stay ahead of the curve.

Although I can attest to those earlier patterns' effectiveness, my compulsive side wanted an emerger pattern that was more in tune with an emerging mayfly. Many times, as a mayfly sheds its nymphal shuck, the shuck is mostly beneath the meniscus of the water, with only the head and wing-bud area above the surface. Most of the emerger patterns I've fished and had success with were tied on straight hooks, with the entire body of the adult and an extended shuck of synthetic material as a tail. Often, trout will key in on this exact phase of the insect's metamorphosis, as it's when they are the most vulnerable. Of course this only applies to those mayflies that emerge in the surface film, but you will often find that patterns tied like this will work for just about any mayfly hatch.

For years I had trouble finding a style of hook that would make a pattern that could imitate this phase of the emergence. Curved grub-style hooks theoretically should've worked, but when cast quickly, they would lie on their side or the shuck would ride on the surface. Then Tiemco engineered a hook that solved this problem. Once the adult emerges from the nymphal shuck, the shuck itself becomes limp and a prisoner to the ebb and flow of the current. Even though the shuck itself is lifeless, it still has lifelike movement. The shuck will actually undulate and shimmy in the water column, and I suspect this can be an important trigger. If you look at effective emerger patterns, you'll see that the shucks on all of them are made from natural or synthetic materials that when wet, closely imitate the color and behavior of the shuck. Often, anglers trying to replicate this with synthetic materials will use too many fibers, causing the shuck to be rigid. The trick is that less is more when working with these fibers, as a little goes a long way.

About 90 percent of the time, I prefer shucks made out of synthetics, as they are relatively inexpensive and are almost always consistent in size, color, and shape. Natural materials, on the other hand, have obvious limitations in those three areas and may yield less usable material when you purchase them. Often, materials like marabou fibers, ostrich herl, or hackle tips can be used for trailing shucks on emergers, but due to a variety of

Angler and Delaware River guide John Miller with a quality brown trout that ate a mayfly emerger. JOHN MILLER

variables are often used only for specific hatches. Ostrich herl, for example, is a nice material for trailing shucks, but is really only a viable option on larger patterns that imitate Drakes due to its larger size. Grizzly hackle tips are a good example of a natural material used in smaller patterns, but they are rigid. Marabou on the other hand is a good option, as it moves freely in water, but what it makes up for in movement, it lacks in durability.

To achieve some sort of proportions in the shuck area of the fly, I needed to add something to the rear portion of the fly that could easily be adapted to other mayfly imitations, regardless of size. A fellow guide-friend and exceptional dry-fly angler, Dave Ingraham once showed me an interesting emerger pattern that he concocted himself. Dave's idea is what inspired me to design the Shucked Up Emerger. Dave's emerger used a shuck tied in a loose bubble around the rear of the fly, and Dave claimed it was his best fly. The pattern in general has required skill to perfect, and I quickly realized that it was good for patterns larger than a size 16, but not easy to replicate on anything smaller.

I wanted some sort of transition zone from the synthetic shuck material and the head of the fly as well as some movement in that area of the fly. If you study an emerging mayfly, you'll notice that a great deal of the movement is right where the adult is splitting the nymphal shuck and trying to shed that exoskeleton in an effort to free itself. I figured if I could somehow mimic this behavior, my emerger pattern might be successful for finicky trout.

Fishing

My first attempts at this pattern were built around the Blue-Winged Olive, most notably the *Baetis* hatch on the legendary Bighorn River, where the Shucked Up Emergers worked well. Once home, I was almost into my own fishing season in the Northeast, and all of the mayfly hatches that came with it. I began frantically tying imitations of all the mayfly hatches I would encounter in the season so as to try my pattern out throughout the duration of the year in hopes that its success was not a fluke. I also made it a point to fish the Shucked Up Emergers in a wide variety of situations. My initial experiment was to fish the Shucked Up Emerger after my first-choice fly pattern began losing its effectiveness. Once a hatch was in full swing and I had landed several fish on any one of my old favorite emerger patterns, I found that the fish would become suspicious of my imitation. When this happened, I would tie on a Shucked Up Emerger in hopes of continued success. As long as my presentations were correct, the fly continued to catch fish. As time wore on, I began to fish nothing but this pattern all season whenever I encountered a mayfly hatch, and I fooled fish on a regular basis. I vividly remember many guide trips that year that ended with my clients asking for some of those "hot emerger patterns" when our time together concluded.

After an entire season had come and gone, I had high confidence in this particular pattern whenever I faced tough trout eating mayflies on the surface. This pattern had become a staple in my dry-fly boxes—one that I would never leave home

A mayfly emerging from its nymphal shuck. As you can see from the photographs, the nymphal shuck is a translucent appendage attached to the tail of the mayfly as it emerges. JOHN MILLER

without—and it accounted for trout of all sizes, including some really nice browns close to 2 feet long. What I later learned was this fly was not just a hatch-only fly pattern; it also worked as a great searching pattern when activity was light or nonexistent. An overdressed Shucked Up Emerger with a bushy wing works exceptionally well fished blind in the riffles and often brings a fish or two to hand when nothing else will. The fly also works well as an indicator in a dry-and-dropper rig, as long as the dropper is not too heavy.

One day while small stream fishing for native brook trout, I brought several dozen fish to hand casting a rusty brown version upstream into the heads of plunge pools and riffles, which elicited violent takes from eager fish below. The best thing about this fly pattern is its durability, as I can catch a fish, either blow off the wing or quickly dress it with floatant, and be back fishing within seconds. Often I can fish several days on the same pattern, and it won't fall apart. Now, whenever I go small stream fishing, I never leave home without a good handful of Shucked Up Emergers in my box.

Mike Klubek holding a fine Delaware brown that fell to a Sulphur yellow Shucked Up Emerger.

Variations

You can replicate virtually all mayfly emergers with this one simple pattern by changing up the wing and body colors. But there are some limitations you must consider. The most noteworthy is the length of the snowshoe hair that you have on hand. Snowshoe rabbits' feet hair can come in a variety of lengths, and your pattern spectrum will be limited by the longest fibers your feet have. Occasionally, I get lucky and find a foot with extraordinarily long fibers, and I can actually tie flies to replicate some of the larger Drake patterns. I will warn you, however, that this is more the exception than the rule, and I have found that flies ranging from a size 10 to 24 are most applicable. Some of my favorite versions of this pattern are based upon many of the medium and small mayfly hatches in the size 16 to 20 range, including Sulphurs, PMDs, Olives, and Blue Quills to name a few.

One of my favorite tricks for achieving a little more realism in these patterns is to use different thread colors and dubbings to match the natural. Take the Eastern Sulphur for example: these particular bugs range in color from bright orange to cream to bright yellow. To easily replicate these bugs when tying them, I simply change the thread color and use the same pale yellow dubbing so I can cover all three colors in one session at the vise.

When I discovered that Tiemco, for some reason, stopped production on the Tiemco 108 SPBL hook, I had some decisions to make. I could easily take any regular length dry-fly hook and simply bend the front section downward at a 45-degree angle as a viable alternative. I ended up tinkering with the Partridge Klinkhamer X-treme hook and never looked back. The size range was much broader and allowed me to replicate even the smallest of mayflies. If I had to go smaller, a trick I learned was to tie the shuck portion shorter on the downward bend of the hook, so as to better imitate size and expose more iron for better hooking capacity.

SULPHUR YELLOW SHUCKED UP EMERGER

Hook: #12-18 Partridge Klinkhamer X-treme
Thread: Yellow 70- or 140-denier Ultra Thread
Shuck: Rust Orangutan Ice Fur and brown ostrich herl
Wing: Cream snowshoe rabbit foot
Legs: March Brown Brahma hen
Thorax: Sulphur orange or pale yellow Superfine Dubbing

Note: You can also use fluorescent orange thread for alternative Sulphur colors.

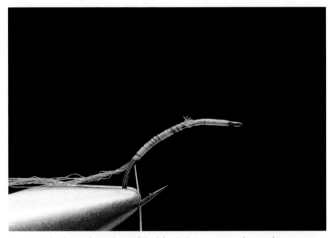

1. Attach the tying thread behind the eye, and continue wrapping rearward to the bend of the hook. Grab a small hank of Ice Fur, and tie it in while keeping the bundle on the top of the hook shank using equal thread pressure to a point just past the hook barb.

3. Start wrapping the bundle of Ice Fur forward toward the tying thread. Do not be overly concerned with making sure that all of the thread wraps are covered. You actually want some of the underbody to bleed through the shuck material. Continue forward and tie off the shuck, being sure to add a half hitch after securing the shuck to prevent it from unwinding between steps.

2. Cut the Ice Fur hank, leaving a trailing shuck about a quarter of the length of the hook shank. Advance the thread to a point just behind the bend of the hook, and reattach the remaining portion of the Ice Fur. Build a tapered cone out of the thread, and advance it to a point just shy of the hook bend.

4. Tie one brown ostrich herl where the Ice Fur shuck ends. Once that's been tied in, advance the thread to the bend and wrap the herl forward. The herl will simulate some movement in the shuck right where the adult portion of the fly is escaping.

5. Cut a small clump of snowshoe rabbit hair from the bottom of a snowshoe rabbit foot. Clean out the underfur with a comb, and then measure the bundle to the hook. The wing should be roughly equal to the length from the hook bend to the trailing shuck.

6. While pinching the wing in your thumb and pointer finger, take a couple of turns of thread around the bundle. Increase the tension downward as you wrap a couple more turns of thread over the bundle.

7. Trim the butt ends that are protruding out over the hook eye on a 45-degree angle toward the eye. This will build the desired taper for the thorax. Add a drop of head cement to the exposed butt ends to help prevent the bundle from rolling.

8. Cover the butt ends with the tying thread, building a nice tapered body. If done correctly, the head should taper to a point behind the hook eye.

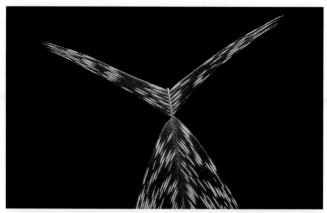

9. Select one Brahma hen feather from a pelt, and remove the tip of the feather. Stroke three or four of the fibers on either side of the stem away from the remainder of the feather.

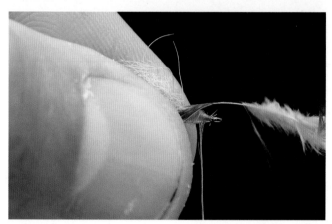

10. Lay the feather over the top of the hook as shown, holding the feather in place with your thumb and pointer finger. Be sure to keep the feather lying on the top of the hook as you secure it with thread wraps. This will ensure that equal fibers remain on either side of the hook.

11. Secure the legs with five or six turns of thread, and trim the stem with your scissors. Once the stem has been trimmed, dub a thin continuous noodle of Superfine Dubbing on your thread. Wrap the dubbing noodle forward toward the eye and whip-finish.

12. Complete the fly by trimming the thread and adding a small drop of head cement or Clear Cure Goo Hydro to the thread wraps.

MARCH BROWN SHUCKED UP EMERGER

Hook: #8-14 Partridge Klinkhamer X-treme
Thread: Tan 140-denier Ultra Thread
Shuck: Rust Orangutan Ice Fur and brown ostrich herl
Wing: Cream snowshoe rabbit foot
Legs: March Brown Brahma hen
Thorax: March Brown Hareline Dubbin or cinnamon caddis
           Superfine Dubbing

SLATE DRAKE SHUCKED UP EMERGER

Hook: #10-14 Partridge Klinkhamer X-treme
Thread: Rusty brown 140-denier Ultra Thread
Shuck: Rust Orangutan Ice Fur and brown ostrich herl
Wing: Dark or medium dun snowshoe rabbit foot
Legs: March Brown Brahma hen
Thorax: Seal brown Hareline Dubbin, or red-brown
           Caucci-Nastasi Spectrumized Dubbing

CHOCOLATE DUN SHUCKED UP EMERGER

Hook: #14-20 Partridge Klinkhamer X-treme
Thread: Dark brown 70- or 140-denier Ultra Thread
Shuck: Rust Orangutan Ice Fur and brown ostrich herl
Wing: Medium dun snowshoe rabbit foot
Legs: March Brown Brahma hen
Thorax: Mahogany brown Superfine Dubbing

DARK HENDRICKSON
SHUCKED UP EMERGER

Hook: #10-14 Partridge Klinkhamer X-treme
Thread: Rusty brown 140-denier Ultra Thread
Shuck: Rust Orangutan Ice Fur and brown ostrich herl
Wing: Medium or light dun snowshoe rabbit foot
Legs: March Brown Brahma hen
Thorax: Seal brown Hareline Dubbin or red-brown
           Caucci-Nastasi Spectrumized Dubbing

PMD
SHUCKED UP EMERGER

Hook: #12-18 Partridge Klinkhamer X-treme
Thread: Cream 70- or 140-denier Ultra Thread
Shuck: Rust Orangutan Ice Fur and brown ostrich herl
Wing: Cream or natural snowshoe rabbit foot
Legs: March Brown Brahma hen
Thorax: Pale Morning Dun or pale yellow Superfine
           Dubbing

BLUE-WINGED OLIVE
SHUCKED UP EMERGER

Hook: #14-20 Partridge Klinkhamer X-treme
Thread: Olive 70- or 140-denier Ultra Thread
Shuck: Rust Orangutan Ice Fur and brown ostrich herl
Wing: Dark or medium dun snowshoe rabbit foot
Legs: March Brown Brahma hen
Thorax: Blue-Winged Olive Superfine Dubbing

CHAPTER 5

Busted Stone

Stoneflies will forever be one of my favorite insects to replicate and fish. Some species grow large, making them a joy to fish as you can see them easily on the surface of the water, and due to their size, they are much easier to construct. Over time, many flies, both suggestive and realistic, have emerged to represent these prehistoric-looking bugs. Although many of the popular patterns are effective and fun to tie, the amount of time put into constructing them often gives anglers a heart-sinking feeling when they lose one.

I never contemplated designing a pattern for these insects until I was fortunate enough to make a trip out West right

The Busted Stone, although built primarily out of a foam body, rides flush in the water as a result of the dubbed underbody. The bushy wing of synthetic and natural hair easily sheds water after each cast.

around Salmonfly season. For years I had always carried a few larger Stimulators in my dry-fly boxes for those few times when I could actually fish a hatch of those bugs. In the Northeast we aren't typically accustomed to the lengthy prolific hatches of larger stones that hatch out West. If you open up many of the fly catalogs every spring, they're filled with dozens and dozens of large stonefly patterns. Most of them are built out of foam and rubber legs, as both materials are readily available in a plethora of colors and sizes, float well, and are relatively inexpensive.

Although foam is a great inexpensive alternative to many natural materials, it lacks movement. You can, however, build a perfect silhouette of whatever you are trying to imitate. When I tie with foam, I prefer to incorporate other materials into the pattern recipe to create a fly that is less static.

I can vividly remember a rainy day at Dave Goulet's fly shop when we were discussing the materials and pattern silhouette. Dave was a genius when it came to this stuff. He tied up a simple Golden Stone out of a single piece of foam and a sparse wing of elk hair. The fly was nothing more than one section of foam cut to the shape of the body, tied in at the head on a shorter-shanked, grub-style hook and a short section of wing. Dave tied up a pair and handed them to me to fish. I had been asking him earlier that day if he had any suggestions on stonefly patterns since I was not up to tying patterns for myself. At the time, I had been witnessing some good emergences of larger Golden Stones and needed something to imitate them.

That evening I went out and fished those two simple flies and caught a bunch of trout, completing my lesson for that day. That simple design was the building block for the stonefly pattern that I would build several years later, and the one that I fish exclusively to this day. I guess you could say I got my inspiration from Dave. His flies have inspired a lot of the designs and tying methods that I use frequently. Because larger Golden Stoneflies are more apt to emerge in the cover of darkness, I remembered this for a later date. Over a ten-year span of guid-

ing, I could count on one hand the number of times I experienced an emergence of these insects during the day. I did, however, on a yearly basis experience the adults depositing their eggs during the day as they dropped out of midair to the water's surface or skittered across the water to dump their precious cargo. These were the times that a surface imitation would work well. But I didn't need a quick pattern to imitate these prehistoric insects until I made a trip out West.

One winter while preparing for a trip to Montana with my good friend, I was tasked with tying up a stonefly pattern that was durable, relatively quick to tie, and floated well. Mike was more apt to just buy a handful of bugs at the local shops once we arrived, but if you know me well, you know that's just something I don't like to do. No offense to the shop owners out there, but I prefer to tie my own, and that's just what I planned on doing. Luckily, I had several months to gather my thoughts and scratch out some ideas on paper before tinkering at the vise. The entire time I was there I couldn't get that pattern out of my head that Dave had given me several years prior. The only problem that I had was it seemed to be missing something. Just what I wasn't sure, but I knew I had to build upon the idea to make it more appealing. Simply put, if my buddies had looked in my box and saw this pattern, they probably would've gotten a good chuckle, as it was pretty much a piece of foam with a clump of deer hair.

To make my efforts quick and easy, I opted to build the foam portion of the fly with the River Road Stonefly Foam Body Cutter set. The kit of cutters makes it easy to replicate the size and shape of a variety of the larger stoneflies. Simply grab your preferred color of foam, and pre-cut all of your bodies ahead of time. I suggest doing this regardless of how many flies you plan on tying, as it saves time and helps prepare in the construction of the fly. One thing I usually do is take an entire sheet of 2-millimeter foam and cut out all the bodies. Whatever I have leftover I place in a Ziploc bag labeled with the body style and size and catalog them away where they are readily accessible for the next time I tie them. Sheets of foam are inexpensive, so I typically purchase mine at my local craft store where I can pick up a sheet that is 12 x 18 inches for under a dollar.

Fishing

By the end of our Montana trip, the Busted Stone held its own and kept right up with all of the local favorites on that trip. One day on the Big Hole, the Busted Stone was getting all of the action even with the high-water conditions.

When I got home, I tied up a pile more of these flies and fished them throughout the summer on my home rivers, and also passed a few handfuls on to my guide buddies. The overall consensus was these flies fished well and held up nicely to a battering of fish throughout the course of a day's work on the water. My good friends, Dan and Tom Harrison of Harrison Outfitters, who specialize in float trips on the Deerfield River in northwestern Massachusetts, are the fly's biggest advocates. I remember Dan asking for a few more of these bugs as he mentioned they had become a favorite searching pattern that particular summer. Tossed into the current seams or softer edges off

A Golden Stonefly adult is a big meal for any trout. Because of their size, replicating these rather complex insects brings a variety of challenges to the fly tier. Merging natural with synthetic materials can accomplish the task. JOHN MILLER

Mike Klubek with a brown that ate a golden-colored Busted Stone cast tight into the brush on the Big Hole River in Montana.

Large high-floating stonefly imitations are good searching patterns on Western freestone rivers and streams like this one in Wyoming, regardless of whether the naturals are hatching at that particular time. MIKE SCHMIDT

of structure while floating, this fly consistently took fish in a variety of water conditions.

When trout are spread out, and the food selection is diverse and bountiful, a well-placed adult stonefly imitation can spark the interest of even the wariest of fish, often bringing some of the larger trout to the surface. They just can't seem to resist such a large meal. This is a tactic that I love to employ in the summer months on my local waters. I'll often spend the day casting to the edges, current seams, and soft edges, prospecting blind for an opportunistic feeder. When I fish this way, I cover large expanses of water in a day as I may take a cast or two to a likely lie and move on. A well-placed cast will often bring a fish up on the first drift or two, and if nobody is home, I move on.

Variations

Without a doubt, Golden Stonefly color combinations are the most prevalent colors that I tie and fish for the Busted Stone, but others for different locations could easily be incorporated into the design. Shades of brown, black, and orange have also worked for me, but as usual, feel free to experiment with color combinations. The palette of colors that you could tie this fly in is diverse, as there are dozens of colors of rabbit dubbing available as well as the color spectrum of foam.

Over time I found that although this pattern uses some buoyant materials, it will sink in the water column in some circumstances. After getting covered with the slime from several fish, or while fishing in heavy current, this fly will have to be redressed with floatant. To make the fly a little more buoyant, I will often tie a few of them with multiple layers of foam as opposed to the single layer of foam. This makes a larger fly, but it will ensure that the fly will float much longer without the need of extra floatant. If I'm concerned that the fly will sink, then I will pre-treat the wing and underwing with some sort of pretreatment like watershed. This little trick will often help the fly clear water and slime from a fish a little easier, meaning the fly will require little dressing between fish and more time floating high on the water.

12. Dub a small, uniform dubbing noodle of Hare-Tron Dubbin, and cover the thread wraps and butt ends of the elk hair. Be sure to start dubbing from the hook eye toward the base of the wing, leaving the tying thread hanging at this point of the fly.

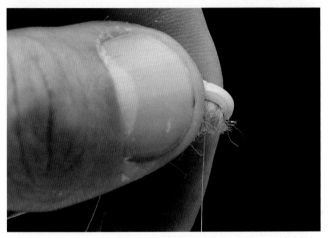

13. While holding with your thumb and pointer finger, fold the section of foam back over the top of the fly to form a bullet head.

14. After securing the bullet head with a few thread wraps, whip-finish and cement the thread wraps. Cut the section of foam at the base of the wing to your liking. I like to have a short tag roughly the same size as the bullet head.

15. Invert the fly in the vise, and brush out the underbody with a piece of velcro or a small dubbing brush. Brush the fibers so that they extend out to either side, creating a buggy underbody. Pull the Flutter Legs together for uniformity and trim them accordingly. Leaving them a little longer will create added motion in the water.

16. The completed fly as seen from the underside. Notice the bugginess created by combing the fibers out.

17. The completed fly as seen from the topside. Notice the underwing is seen through the overwing. The key is to not over-dress the wing in general so that the underwing shines through.

18. The completed fly as seen upright in the vise. Notice the rough underside of the body of the fly.

ORANGE BUSTED STONE

Hook: #6-12 Tiemco 2302
Thread: Burnt orange 140-denier Ultra Thread
Underbody: Burnt orange Hareline Hare-Tron Dubbin
Overbody: Orange foam body (2 mm)
Legs: Root beer Hareline Grizzly Flutter Legs
Underwing: Quick Silver EP Trigger Point Fibers
Overwing: Natural elk
Head: Orange foam (2 mm)

Note: This is a double foam body version of the pattern, which is used for heavier water to aid in floatation.

BROWN BUSTED STONE

Hook: #6-12 Tiemco 2302
Thread: Dark Brown 140-denier Ultra Thread
Underbody: Dark brown Hareline Hare-Tron Dubbin
Overbody: Brown foam body (2 mm)
Legs: Root beer Hareline Grizzly Flutter Legs
Underwing: Quick Silver EP Trigger Point Fibers
Overwing: Natural elk
Head: Brown foam (2 mm)

CHAPTER 6

Tiny Dancer Caddis Pupa

Challenging days can be some of the most rewarding if you take the time to be observant and study what is bringing you difficulty. Some of my toughest days fishing have resulted in some of my greatest discoveries. This variety of challenges is one of the biggest draws of fly fishing.

Dolophilodes distinctus, the Winter/Summer Caddis that inhabits my homewaters of the Farmington River, is one of the most important and prolific hatches of the watershed. This minuscule insect draws a tremendous amount of attention from trout. The insect is referred to as the Winter/Summer Caddis but in actuality it could easily be called the All-Season Caddis, as it can emerge any day of the year. What's distinctive about this

Tiny Dancer Caddis is a miniature extended body pattern designed to imitate a specific surface-oriented caddis pupa.

The Female Winter Caddis Pupa, a miniscule insect that can bring large trout to the surface to feed. These small but important insects are much more widespread than anglers think. I have fished hatches of them on a variety of tailwater fisheries across the Northeast.

particular insect is that the female pupa is wingless and scurries across the water's surface to find a male counterpart to mate with. It is fairly common during heavy periods of hatch activity to witness hundreds of both genders dancing around on the rocks in a sort of mating ritual. The winged males with their speckled brownish wings will often flutter and dance around in circles to attract a viable mate while the females dance around in the same manner.

Although the winged males will get eaten by trout from time to time, the wingless females get the bulk of the attention as they make the dash toward the shoreline. Somehow, the trout of the Farmington have recognized the vulnerability of these tiny insects, strategically positioning themselves in the paths of the females to intercept them before they reach their destinations. Many times, these little bugs are intercepted inches from the shoreline, especially in shallow areas right off the bank of the river. A riseform to these caddis is usually easy to identify, as they can often be violent, splashy slurps on the surface.

In late fall and early winter, these little insects have the tendency to hatch in the morning, often right at daybreak, but depending on the weather, may emerge at any given time throughout the day. If you're fishing on the Farmington and happen to be experiencing rises near the shoreline, take a closer look and you may find that these insects are emerging. You have to pay close attention, however, as they are an elusive bug ranging in size from 18 to 22, in shades of black, brown, or amber, making them at times difficult to see.

For years this hatch stumped many, and as the legend goes, anglers found periodic success with a variety of concoctions, but nothing ever seemed to work consistently. Over time, a group of anglers spearheaded by David Goulet, the owner of the late Classic and Custom Fly Shop, put their minds together and came up with the Foam Caddis Emerger, which has become a staple pattern for this hatch. This pattern is synonymous with

the Farmington River, and pretty much anyone you ask about flies for this watershed will put this fly at the top of the list.

The pattern itself isn't especially noteworthy; it is the manner of fishing that sets it apart. The same people who designed the pattern also developed a specific technique to mimic the race of the wingless pupa across the surface. Some call it the shimmy, wiggle, or caddis dance; whatever you call it, it often results in a bent rod and a happy angler once you've mastered it. To effectively replicate this behavior, a slight steady but slow lift of the rod tip makes the fly migrate across the surface. Some incorporate a slow side-to-side wiggle of the rod to imitate the scurrying nature of the insect as they skate in short bursts. One thing to keep in mind is you don't want to do this too deliberately or quickly; if the fly begins to wake, you need to slow it down.

On many days, this is the only tactic that will consistently take trout feeding on these insects, while other days, a dead-drifted imitation will work. Experience has taught me to fish a manipulated imitation first and let the trout tell you how they like it. If you can't buy a fish on a skated or wiggled imitation, first make sure that you aren't waking the fly on the retrieve. If that is not the case, then resort to a dead-drift presentation and you should start picking up a fish or two. In a worst-case scenario, the trout may in fact be keying in on the winged males, so as a last-ditch effort, a brown-colored R-F Caddis or Elk Hair Caddis will suffice.

Now, you're probably wondering why I've mentioned so much about a pattern I had no part in designing. But the Foam Caddis Emerger gave me inspiration to formulate a secondary pattern for times when the trout are super selective. The Tiny Dancer Caddis Pupa was by far one of my longest endeavors to date of trying to fine-tune a pattern that was not only effective, but relatively easy to tie. I can't think of another fly pattern where I went back to the drawing board more often. In fact, due

The Foam Caddis Pupa in its original recipe as devised by Dave Goulet and several members of the Farmington River Anglers Association. The simple design using a foam cylinder, hen hackle, and dubbing is a proven pattern that many fishermen have had success with every season.

to frustration I walked away from this pattern for the better part of five years, as I had given up on the notion that I could come up with something new. In the end, a new tool hit the tying market that changed my thinking and helped me come up with the exact design that I was looking for: J:son's Detached Body Pins.

Extended body dry flies are a style of fly that has forever given me fits. I always loved the way they looked, but was an amateur at best in their construction. It wasn't until I received a set of J:son's Detached Body Pins that I realized there was hope in building an extended body version of this fly. The body pin is a brilliant system designed for building extended body patterns. Essentially, they are nothing more than a section of slightly bent wire with a spring attached to one end.

After several days of tinkering with this awesome little device, I realized that I could actually make extended body patterns for small flies. After a long hiatus, I finally had an idea to create a pattern for the Winter Caddis. By using small, thinly cut strips of 2-millimeter foam, I could erect the bodies of a fly with ease while also creating some segmentation at the same time.

Fishing

Patterns designed to solve a problem often require a distinctive fishing style, and the Tiny Dancer Caddis is no different. Like the Foam Caddis Emerger, the Tiny Dancer Caddis is a pattern that works well when danced or skated across the surface of the water. Manipulating the tip of the rod in a slight side-to-side wiggling action with extra care to not wake the fly, will often be the best way to catch fish. This technique is most effective when fishing across stream, working the fly back toward the river's edge as it drifts downstream with the current. When fish are actively feeding on the pupae, casting the fly several feet from the riseform and working the fly in this manner into the trout's feeding lane will usually result in a take.

If your efforts are being refused, switch up to a dead-drift, drag-free presentation. Sometimes the trout will respond better this way, but more often they prefer a moving target, as it more closely represents the action of the natural. You can fish this particular pattern anytime a Winter or Summer Caddis hatch is prevalent, but I usually turn to this pattern when trout are refusing my Foam Caddis Emerger.

What's nice about this pattern is it has a higher vertical profile than the Foam Caddis Emerger, which makes it a little easier to track on the water's surface. The hackles and extended foam body ride in the film, but are exposed enough to make it more visible on the surface. If you can't see the pattern, then I suggest tying it on a short dropper behind a more visible dry fly, but keep the tippet relatively short.

The first winter I fished this particular pattern was very successful. I made a conscious effort to fish both the Foam Caddis Emerger and Tiny Dancer Caddis either in tandem or alone, giving each equal amounts of time on the water to truly test the two side by side. I kept a journal that entire year of my efforts, and in the end the results were astonishingly similar: the Foam Caddis Emerger fooled sixty-seven fish while the Tiny Dancer

Caddis fooled sixty-six. To this day I make sure that I tie up a handful of both flies every season and replenish my supply when it gets low.

Because takes from trout for these flies can be violent, break offs are common. To avoid losing too many flies, I will typically fish 5X or 6X tippet, as it gives me a little more strength. If you speak with many of the regulars on my home waters who fish this hatch, you will often hear them speak of how you just can't get a trout to eat unless you're fishing 8X or 9X tippet. This is not true, and more often than not, it's unnecessary. A loop knot allows the fly to move more freely on the water's surface, even with heavier tippet.

It is in the trout's best interest that we use the heaviest tippet possible, as this cuts down on the possibility of overplaying a fish, something that lighter tackle can unfortunately do when fighting large fish. A good rule of thumb is to use the heaviest tippet that still allows you to successfully fool trout. Someday, while you're on the water and having success, experiment with this concept, you might be surprised at how heavy you can go before the trout stop eating your fly. Usually presentation is what's lacking, not the diameter of the tippet. Spend more time practicing better presentations and less time fiddling with lighter tackle. In the long run, it will improve your skills while also helping aid sound catch-and-release practices.

Variations

In the beginning, the only two variations to this fly pattern were simply a matter of colors. The bodies of the Winter Caddis are either a shade of brown or grayish black, and these were the only two colors that I would replicate. In time, however, I recognized that the pattern could be adapted for a variety of winged caddis imitations as well, and I quickly began tinkering with different colors and sizes with the addition of a wing. If you're looking for a good pattern to skate across the surface during times when caddis are depositing eggs, this particular design works well.

The choice of wing material is up to you. Personally, I like either snowshoe rabbit foot fur or CDC, but elk or deer hair will work equally well. I spent the summer after I created this fly experimenting with skated winged versions of it after I came up with the final design of this pattern. I had some trying times a couple of evenings in succession that led me to play around with a winged version of this pattern. That following spring while on the water, I witnessed many *Brachycentrus* caddis dapping and dancing on the surface of the water while they deposited their eggs. Among these dancing caddis were eruptive rises by trout. Some of the trout rocketed themselves completely out of the water, and even large trout were taking part in this activity. After a couple of nights with little success to show for it, I went home and began brainstorming. Having never been on the water when this had happened before, but being readily familiar with the scenario from various pieces of fishing literature that I had read over the years, I decided that I better have some flies like the Tiny Dancer Caddis in case I ran into this situation again. (In a pinch, the Tiny Dancer is a good imitation for an ant.)

BROWN TINY DANCER CADDIS PUPA

Hook: #16-20 Tiemco 206 BL
Thread: Rusty brown 70-denier Ultra Thread
Body: Brown foam extended body (2 mm)
Legs: Brown Hareline Daddy Long Legs
Hackle: Black hen feather
Dubbing: Tan CDC feather fibers

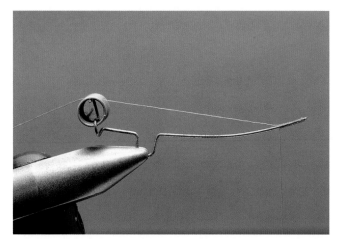

1. Affix a J:son Detached Body pin into the jaws of the vise and wrap a course of thread down the first ½ inch of the pin. Be sure to leave an extra long tag of thread to cover and affix in the spring section of the body pin.

2. Cut a thin slice from a section of 2-millimeter foam with a razor blade and ruler. Make the slice roughly ¹⁄₁₆ inch. You can cut several ahead of time to prepare to build the extended bodies.

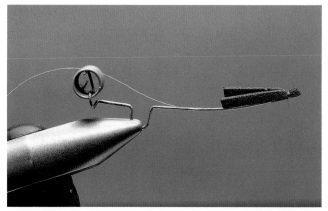

3. Return your tying thread to a point a few turns of thread in from the end of the pin. Fold the foam around the end of the body pin and wrap two or three turns of thread over the foam. Then half hitch the thread so that it won't come undone.

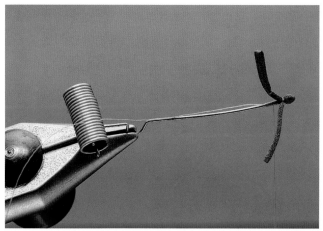

4. After completing the half hitch, advance your thread forward on the body pin, flaring out the foam. Advance the thread forward two or three turns, or to a point that is equal distance from the end of the foam to the first set of thread wraps. Repeat the prior step to create a second section in the foam.

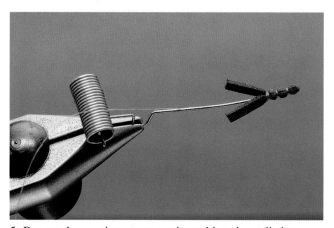

5. Repeat the previous steps again making three distinct segments in the foam body. When completed, whip-finish and cement the thread wraps over the foam, then remove the extended body from the pin, leaving the long tag end of thread.

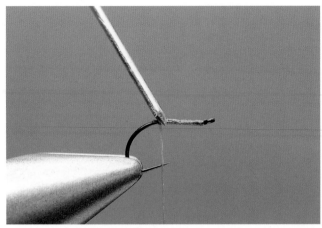

6. Affix the hook in the vise, tie a course of thread to a point just shy of the bend of the hook, and add a small drop of head cement or Zap-A-Gap to the thread wraps.

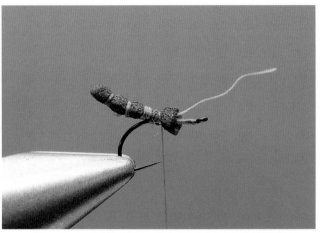

7. Attach the extended body to the top of the hook with a couple of turns of thread, being sure to keep the body on the top of the hook.

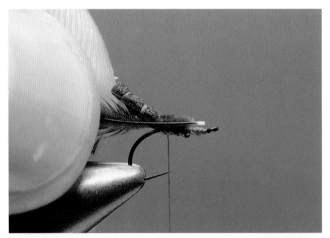

8. Further secure the body to the top of the hook with four to six more turns of thread, and trim the tag end of thread. Take a black hen feather from a dyed hen cape, and trim the fibers shorter on either side of the stem. This will ensure that once lashed to the hook it will not pull out easily when wrapped.

9. After securing the hen feather, tie in a pair of Daddy Long Legs on either side of the hook, as illustrated on page 10 of the R-F Caddis chapter.

10. Select one cul de canard feather with longer, fuller fibers as seen in the picture.

11. Grab a few fibers from the CDC feather, and twist them onto the tying thread in the same manner that you would twist a dubbing noodle, and begin covering the thread wraps on the front portion of the fly.

12. Spiral-wrap the hen feather through the dubbed portion of the fly, and then tie it off, trim the excess, and whip-finish the thread. Cement the head with your choice of cement. Trim the legs and antennae to length, being mindful to leave the legs a little longer than the front antennae.

BLACK TINY DANCER CADDIS PUPA

Hook:	#16-20 Tiemco 206 BL
Thread:	Black 70-denier Ultra Thread
Body:	Black foam extended body (2 mm)
Legs:	Brown Hareline Daddy Long Legs
Hackle:	Black hen feather
Dubbing:	Tan CDC feather fibers

AMBER TINY DANCER CADDIS PUPA

Hook:	#16-20 Tiemco 206 BL
Thread:	Tan 70-denier Ultra Thread
Body:	Amber foam extended body (2 mm)
Legs:	Brown Hareline Daddy Long Legs
Hackle:	Black hen feather
Dubbing:	Black CDC feather fibers

PART II
Nymphs

CHAPTER 7

Designing Nymphs

Day in and day out, the most consistent way to catch trout is through fishing nymphs. For better or for worse, nymph-fishing tactics seasonally account for 60 to 75 percent of my time spent guiding for various reasons. Let's face it, if you're on the water for the better part of the day, you may not see many fish feeding on the surface, especially during periods without hatch activity. To fill the time and keep rods bent, you'd better know how to fish subsurface, or it's going to be a long day on the water for you and your client. And if you're the type of angler who likes to constantly catch fish, nymph fishing is hands down best way to accomplish this. Research shows that in some fisheries surface fare may make up less than 15 to 20 percent of a trout's daily diet, and even less on some watersheds.

Angler Jeff Dixon landing a brown trout that fell for a DDT nymph. Well-presented nymph patterns are some of the most effective patterns to fish day in and day out.

many situations, but when you fish a river where pressured trout see hundreds of Pheasant Tails in a week, it's good to have a viable alternative.

The DT spawned as a variation of Andy Burk's Hunchback Baetis. I remember when I first fished Andy's pattern, I really liked the way it looked and how effective it was. The overall proportions of the fly, like many small imitations, were far larger than many of the smaller mayfly nymphs that I encountered on my home waters, and it continued to bother the compulsive side of my fly-tying psyche.

Although the pattern yielded fish under most conditions, its effectiveness would taper off when the fish were picky or the hatches were smaller than size 18. What I also found with the pattern was that the flash ribbing would break after a few fish, and the legs and tail, even though they looked realistic, were just not as durable as I wanted them to be.

Often, when designing patterns to replicate smaller insects, it's easiest to scale down some of the larger imitations that you have confidence in. Even though this seems like a logical solution, unfortunately, it often leads to a fly with an oversize profile. Let's dissect this a bit further and look at ribbing, for example. Although we have a much wider variety of wire sizes on the market, some tiny in diameter, often the ribbing material can cause bumps in the body of the fly, which on smaller flies may affect how the pattern rides in the water column—never mind the misshapen appearance. Other materials such as Mylar Flash or Krystal Flash, for example, may provide less bulk in the construction of the pattern, but the trade-off is they are not nearly as durable and will often unravel or tear after only a couple of fish.

The answer was simple: eliminate the ribbing material entirely, and see what the fish thought once I completed the fly. But it took time before I figured this out, as my initial attempts used flash as a rib. Although the pattern was thin and streamlined, the flash ribbing could not withstand the teeth of even the smallest trout. Natural tail and leg materials can have the same problems. However, while synthetic materials do not duplicate some of the characteristics of natural materials, they do provide fantastic durability to flies that most natural materials cannot equal.

Often, when tying smaller flies, natural materials have limitations beyond a lack of durability. Size is the most common issue, as smaller feathers, for example, are not abundant and often difficult to work with. Legs and tails require you to improvise at times, and you'll often have to cut short natural materials like partridge or hen feathers just to keep the pattern in proportion with the hook that they are tied on. What will often happen is you end up wasting two-thirds to three-quarters of the feather after it is tied in place when trimming away the excess, rendering the rest of the feather unusable.

At the time of my revelation with this pattern, I had recently discovered the synthetic material Darlon. Darlon is a thin, shiny, silky fiber that comes in a hank for a couple of dollars. The manufacturer offers the material in a large variety of shades, and at the time that I was introduced to it, several fly tiers were already using the material for wings on dries, posts for parachutes, or underwings on many other variations of winged adults.

The DT Nymph is the same pattern recipe as the DDT, but without a bead.

Determining what style of hook to tie this pattern on was fairly easy. On my initial attempts, I used a Tiemco 2487, primarily because of the hook's curved, scudlike appearance. But I wasn't fond of the limited gap space on that hook once it got smaller than a size 18. In due time, I decided to use a couple of different styles of hooks. On anything down to a size 18, I prefer the Tiemco 2499 SPBL, which is a fantastic scud-style hook. If I have to tie anything smaller, I use a Tiemco 2488, as it has ample gap, the shape is ideal for smaller nymphs, and the wire is a little thicker than the 206 BL which is also a viable option.

The next step was finding a body material that would avoid any of the proportion issues. My first thought was to build a tapered body out of thread only, but I wasn't a big fan of the final product, which was too rigid and lacked texture. I wanted something a little more lifelike. The solution was easy: use

Darlon is a much finer and softer synthetic fiber than many of its brother materials, making it a perfect ingredient for smaller nymph patterns.

Superfine Dubbing. Superfine Dubbing is probably one of the finest, softest, easiest materials to spin onto tying thread, and it comes in dozens of colors. It's often used to construct medium and small dry-fly patterns.

Superfine Dubbing was the obvious choice, and I soon learned that the appearance of the fly can easily be altered by using different thread colors. Simply use a darker thread color with lighter dubbing to achieve the desired effect. To test this theory, dub a small noodle of light olive–colored dubbing on a brown-colored thread, apply a little moisture, and see what happens.

Once I managed to configure the pattern, I put it to the test on my local waters the next day. Yet again, I was lucky to experience a thick emergence of *Ephemerella needhami* mayflies. I suspended a pair of these nymphs in a size 18 under a tiny split shot and yarn indicator, targeting the faster runs and transitions zones at the heads of a few pools.

The flies' initial ventures were fairly successful, fooling a good number of brown and rainbow trout in the 12 to 16 inch range, and continued to do so for the next few weeks. The next

season came, but I still wasn't satisfied with the overall appearance of the fly, so I took it back to the drawing board again to try and finalize the pattern. The fly worked fairly well, but something was definitely missing.

One evening, I was using Midge Flash for a ribbing material on some of these flies, nearly giving in to my doubts, and telling myself that I would have to live with this pattern only holding up after a couple of fish. As I clipped off the tag end of the flash on the fly I was tying, I put the remainder of the Midge Flash on my bench. Upon doing so, I inadvertently dropped it in the pile of Darlon that I was using for the wing case and legs. My error ended up answering my prayers. After tying in the Darlon and Midge Flash and dubbing the abdomen of the fly, I pulled the Darlon and Midge Flash wing case over and tied it off.

The fly came to life when the light from my desk lamp hit the Midge Flash that was now draped across the top of the fly. I liked what I saw, but I felt it could be improved even further. I took the fly out of the vise, replaced it with a bare hook, and started over, this time, omitting the flashy rib and tying in two pieces of Midge Flash underneath the Darlon. After dubbing the abdomen, I pulled the Midge Flash and Darlon over the top, tied it off, and then separated one strand of the Midge Flash to either side with the separated Darlon for the legs of the fly. Now the fly was complete, and the next day that exact pattern made a name for itself in those riffles I had fished the day prior.

Fishing

The DT Nymph was intended as a dropper fly in an indicator nymph system. As I stated earlier, I wanted a smaller mayfly imitation that was quick to tie, effective, and easily altered by changing colors of materials to cover a wide variety of smaller mayfly nymphs.

As a dropper in an indicator rig, this pattern excels. I like to spread my nymphs out approximately 18 inches apart by placing the larger of the two flies above the smaller fly. In this particular case, the DT is the dropper about 95 percent of the time unless I'm fishing it in tandem with a smaller fly or another DT. Typically, I place my split shot above the pair, usually anywhere from 8 to 18 inches from the lead fly. I'm typically fishing the DT Nymph in the thick of the season, when flows are more stable and insect diversity and availability are both high, so I may not even have to pair the DT with a larger searching pattern.

Sometimes I may be fishing a pair in tandem, usually in two different color schemes, until I find the color that the fish are responding to. Once I dial in the right size and color, I'll fish a pair until they stop working. If I need them to get deep fast, I will fish the DDT as a lead fly with a DT dropper, as the DDT will anchor the pattern a little better in the water column and help the pair get down faster.

The DT is also effectively fished as a dropper behind a dry fly. Often, when trout are feeding on smaller emerging nymphs in the upper part of the water column, it's deadly to fish a DT 8 to 18 inches below a buoyant dry-fly pattern, usually something with a snowshoe rabbit wing or deer or elk hair. A Snowshoe

Tiny mayfly nymphs require minimal amounts of material to represent, as seen in these small nymphs. JOHN MILLER

A solid brown trout that ate a dead-drifted DDT Nymph. Trout of all sizes, even large ones, will eat small nymph patterns. Never under-estimate the fish-catching ability of a fly just because of its size.

Emerger, my Shucked Up Emerger, or any style of buoyant foam-based pattern will usually do the trick. If the dry fly sinks or darts in the water column, set the hook, as you're most likely attached to a fish.

When the fish become ultra selective, then your best bet is to attach your DT dropper to a fly similar in size to optimize your ability to catch fish. What I often do with my droppers is tie a section of fluorocarbon from the dry fly to the dropper. I do this for a couple of reasons, mostly because the fluorocarbon will break the surface tension and sink quicker, but also because it refracts less light and so trout supposedly can't see it. To aid in the DT's sink rate, degrease the dropper tippet with Snake River Mud, or just plain old mud from the stream bottom. This is also an underused trick for fishing dry flies, and is a must with all new tapered leaders. This will increase your ability to present your fly without drag, as it removes the oil from the leader.

Over the years, I've found that there are some specific mayfly hatches where the DT does well. Aside from the *Ephemerella needhami* hatch on the Farmington, various Sulphurs, Blue-Winged Olives, and PMD nymphs can be easily imitated.

Due to the wide variety of Sulphurs that we experience in the Northeast, especially on our spring creeks and tailwaters, it's wise to carry the DT in a variety of sizes, usually from size 16 down to 22. If you are tying these yourself and only want one size, the best option is size 18, as it will cover most situations and is one of the most prevalent sizes the trout see. Many days, a size 18 DT in mahogany and orange has tempted trout when not much else would.

Variations

The DT Nymph has become a staple small fly imitation for me and many of my guide clients and fly customers. The fly's simplicity makes it a great pattern for a beginning fly tier as well, and it is one of the patterns that I habitually include in any fly-tying class that I teach.

Like all good things, the pattern has continued to evolve. With the advent of UV curing resins like Clear Cure Goo Hydro, the DT Nymph has become even more irresistible to trout and more durable, too. Now, when I tie up a batch of DT Nymphs, I place a drop of Clear Cure Goo Hydro over the wing case and cure it with the UV torch. This little step serves two purposes: it adds more durability to an already solid pattern, and it also alters the color of the Darlon wing case, typically making it darker, reminiscent of the darker-colored wing buds of the natural insects prior to emergence.

In time I realized that I needed to tie this particular fly with some added weight so that it could be used in some of the European-style or tight-line, nymph-fishing situations. This is easy as 1.5- and 2.0-millimeter tungsten beads are available in a slew of colors, so the simple addition of a bead head can help achieve more weight.

I not only found that this particular version was deadly in a long-leader Spanish or French nymphing setup as a dropper or ultralight anchor, but also that it was effective as a dropper off of a medium or large dry fly when prospecting edges in the summer. Long-leader, tight-line rigs are precise ways to fish smaller weighted flies from a distance on pressured fisheries. When trout key in on smaller fare in clear conditions, being able to fish shallow water from a distance is beneficial, and these particular flies are good candidates for those methods. On several occasions, the DDT has saved the day when nothing else would. Don't be fooled by this particular pattern's minuscule size, as it will habitually fool fish in excess of 20 inches every season.

BROWN DDT NYMPH

Hook:	#16-20 Tiemco 2499 SPBL
Bead:	Copper tungsten
Thread:	Dark brown 70-denier Ultra Thread
Tail:	Brown Darlon
Abdomen:	Brown Hareline Superfine or Microfine Dubbing
Thorax:	Brown Hareline Superfine or Microfine Dubbing
Wing Case/Legs:	Brown Darlon and root beer Midge Flash
Hot Spot:	Hot orange Datum Glo Brite (optional)

Note: For the bead, use 1.5 mm for #20, 2.0 mm for #18, and 2.5 mm for #16.

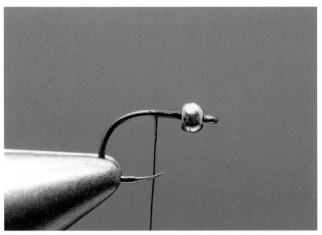

1. Slide a bead over the hook and place it in the jaws of the vise. Attach the tying thread, and begin wrapping directly behind the bead to a point about midway down the hook shank.

2. Remove a small bundle of roughly fifteen fibers from a hank of Darlon. Tie them in at the midway point of the hook with four or five turns of thread keeping the bundle on top of the hook. Once you have made those few wraps, pull the bundle gently to bring the butt ends to the first couple of thread wraps while maintaining pressure on the thread. This will waste the least amount of material.

3. Continue wrapping the thread deep into the midway point of the hook bend. Lightly dub a thin tapered noodle of Superfine Dubbing to the thread and begin winding the noodle forward.

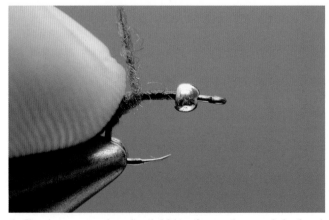

4. Continue wrapping the dubbing forward toward the bead. You can use the thumb of your free hand to preen the dubbing rearward as you wind it up the hook. This helps build the taper of any errant fibers.

5. Dub the noodle to a point approximately at the midpoint of the hook beak, and half hitch your thread so that it doesn't unwind on you. Trim your tail so that it is roughly the length of your dubbed abdomen.

8. Dub a slightly thicker uniform noodle of Superfine Dubbing to your tying thread to build the thorax. Wind the noodle forward toward the bead, and let your thread hang behind the bead.

6. Add a single strand of Midge Flash to the remaining bundle of Darlon from the tail, and secure it to the top of the hook. Be sure to tie the materials in, leaving a section over the bead.

9. Pull your Darlon and Midge Flash bundles over the top of the fly to form your wing case, and secure the two bundles with three or four thread wraps.

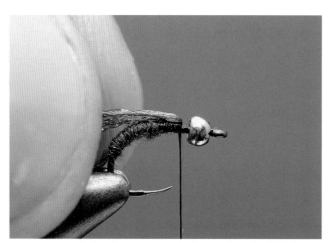

7. Fold rearward the bundle of Darlon and Midge Flash that is currently facing forward, and secure it with your tying thread. Be sure to wrap the thread back to the point where the abdomen ends, and then half hitch the thread again so that it doesn't pull out.

10. Separate the two bundles while maintaining pressure on your tying thread. Pull one bundle of Darlon and one section of Midge Flash to the near side of the hook, and secure it with three or four thread wraps. The bundle should face rearward at a 45-degree angle to the shank.

11. Do the same on the far side with the other section of Darlon and remaining section of Midge Flash.

12. Do a four- or five-turn whip-finish making a neat collar of thread directly behind the bead and trim your thread. You can add a thin layer of head cement to the thread wraps and trim the legs. The best way to ensure that your legs are uniform in length is to grab the two sections and pull them upward and trim them together so that they are $1/3$ the length of the fly.

13. (Optional.) Attach your hot spot material directly over the thread wraps behind the bead. After completing four or five turns, whip-finish the hot spot and clip the thread.

14. With a bodkin, place a small drop of head cement or Clear Cure Goo Hydro or other thin UV resin over the wing case and hot spot collar and cure. Notice how this darkens the wing case.

15. The completed fly with noticeable darker wing case. As you can see from the photo, the overall proportion of the fly is slim like many of the smaller mayfly nymphs you would encounter in nature.

BWO DDT NYMPH

Hook: #16-20 Tiemco 2499 SPBL
Bead: Nickel tungsten
Thread: Olive 70-denier Ultra Thread
Tail: Rusty Brown Darlon
Abdomen: Blue Wing Olive Hareline Superfine or Microfine Dubbing
Thorax: Baetis gray Hareline Microfine Dubbing
Wing Case/Legs: Olive Darlon and olive Midge Flash
Hot Spot: Chartreuse Datum Glo Brite (optional)

Note: For the bead, use 1.5 mm for #20, 2.0 mm for #18, and 2.5 mm for #16.

SULPHUR DDT NYMPH

Hook: #16-20 Tiemco 2499 SPBL
Bead: Copper tungsten
Thread: Rusty brown 70-denier Ultra Thread
Tail: Rusty brown Darlon
Abdomen: Rusty brown Hareline Superfine or Microfine Dubbing
Thorax: Sulphur orange or yellow Hareline Superfine or Microfine Dubbing
Wing Case/Legs: Rusty brown Darlon and root beer Midge Flash
Hot Spot: Hot orange Datum Glo Brite (optional)

Note: For the bead, use 1.5 mm for #20, 2.0 mm for #18, and 2.5 mm for #16.

OLIVE/BROWN DDT NYMPH

Hook: #16-20 Tiemco 2499 SPBL
Bead: Gold tungsten
Thread: Olive brown 70-denier Ultra Thread
Tail: Olive Darlon
Abdomen: Olive-brown Hareline Superfine or Microfine Dubbing
Thorax: Olive-brown Hareline Superfine or Microfine Dubbing
Wing Case/Legs: Olive Darlon and olive Midge Flash
Hot Spot: Chartreuse Datum Glo Brite (optional)

Note: For the bead, use 1.5 mm for #20, 2.0 mm for #18, and 2.5 mm for #16.

DARK BROWN DDT NYMPH

Hook:	#16-20 Tiemco 2499 SPBL
Bead:	Black tungsten
Thread:	Dark brown 70-denier Ultra Thread
Tail:	Dark brown Darlon
Abdomen:	Mahogany brown Hareline Superfine or Microfine Dubbing
Thorax:	Mahogany brown Hareline Superfine or Microfine Dubbing
Wing Case/Legs:	Dark brown Darlon and root beer Midge Flash
Hot Spot:	Hot pink Datum Glo Brite (optional)

Note: For the bead, use 1.5 mm for #20, 2.0 mm for #18, and 2.5 mm for #16.

MEDIUM BWO DDT NYMPH

Hook:	#16-20 Tiemco 2499 SPBL
Bead:	Nickel tungsten
Thread:	Olive 70-denier Ultra Thread
Tail:	Medium dun Darlon
Abdomen:	BWO Gray Olive Hareline Superfine or Microfine Dubbing
Thorax:	Gray Olive Hareline Microfine Dubbing
Wing Case/Legs:	Olive Darlon and olive Midge Flash
Hot Spot:	Chartreuse Datum Glo Brite (optional)

Note: For the bead, use 1.5 mm for #20, 2.0 mm for #18, and 2.5 mm for #16.

The DDT Nymph is a simple and efficiently constructed fly pattern that requires minimal amount of tying expertise. Even a novice tier can fill several rows of a fly box in short order.

CHAPTER 9

Slasher

Midges are some of the most prolific insects in a trout stream, and on some rivers, particularly tailwaters, they make up the bulk of a trout's diet. No matter what part of the country you live in, trout eat midges, and they account for varying amounts of their diet. In many rivers and streams, these little bugs are the only insects readily available in the winter months when all other insects lie dormant. In some rivers, trout will eat midge larva imitations regularly even when they aren't drifting freely in the water column. Midge larvae have been known to drift in the current at any time of day and at any time of the year, making them a prevalent food source for trout regardless of their size. Midges are important for stillwater anglers as well.

This size 22 Slasher fooled a spectacular cutbow.
LANDON MAYER

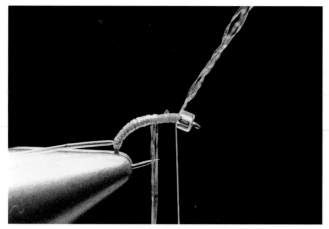

6. Grab the three strands of Krystal Flash at the rear of the fly, and begin wrapping them forward toward the bead.

7. Tie off the Krystal Flash and force it upright with a couple of extra thread wraps behind the now six strands of Krystal Flash. This will prop the materials upright.

8. Wrap over the Krystal Flash with the Micro Tubing, and tie it off behind the upright Krystal Flash wing. Be sure to put a half hitch in the thread before starting the next step, or else the tubing could pull free and unravel.

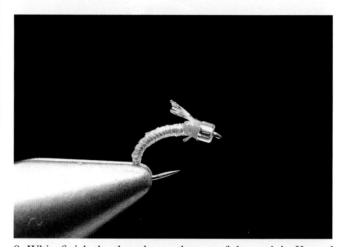

9. Whip-finish the thread over the top of the upright Krystal Flash wing. This will force the wing to rest rearward over the back of the fly. Trim the wing with your scissors evenly so that it is approximately half the length of the hook gap. Cement the thread wraps and the fly is complete.

DARK SLASHER (CHOCOLATE THUNDER)

Hook: #16-24 Tiemco 2487 BL
Bead: Brown or gunmetal glass (1.5 or 2 mm)
Thread: Black 70-denier Ultra Thread
Underbody: Black Krystal Flash
Overbody: Gray Hareline Micro Tubing
Wing: Black Krystal Flash

Note: You can substitute any similar barbless scud hook.

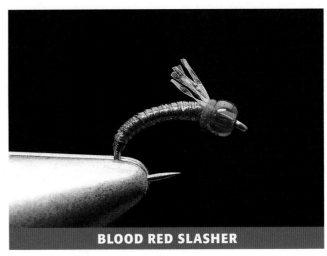

BLOOD RED SLASHER

Hook: #16-24 Tiemco 2487 BL
Bead: Red glass (1.5 or 2 mm)
Thread: Red 70-denier Ultra Thread
Underbody: Pearl Krystal Flash
Overbody: Blood red Hareline Micro Tubing
Wing: Pearl Krystal Flash

Note: You can substitute any similar barbless scud hook.

OLIVE SLASHER

Hook: #16-24 Tiemco 2487 BL
Bead: Glass (1.5 or 2 mm)
Thread: Gray-brown 70-denier Ultra Thread
Underbody: Pearl Krystal Flash
Overbody: Olive Hareline Micro Tubing
Wing: Pearl Krystal Flash

Note: You can substitute any similar barbless scud hook.

WEIGHTED SLASHER

Hook: #16-24 Tiemco 2487 BL
Bead: Silver tungsten (1.5 or 2 mm)
Thread: Hot orange 70-denier Ultra Thread
Underbody: Pearl Krystal Flash
Overbody: Clear Hareline Micro Tubing
Wing: Pearl Krystal Flash

Note: You can substitute any similar barbless scud hook.

CHAPTER 10

Infant Stone

Though overlooked by many anglers, tiny stonefly nymphs are not overlooked by trout. During milder winters when conditions are conducive to fishing, they are important to the trout's diet. (During harsher winters, they hatch readily and crawl on the snow and ice, but the rivers may not be fishable.) In many winters while eagerly awaiting spring, I have seen thousands of Winter Stonefly nymphs wiggle and writhe through the water column to either hatch or make their way to the shoreline. Many of the existing patterns that imitate the smaller Winter Stoneflies, which hatch in February and March in the Northeast, have incorrect proportions, mostly in the tails and body. I was convinced that I needed a fly pattern that not

Imitations of smaller nymphs need not be complicated. The Infant Stone incorporates a minimal amount of materials to achieve a very effective pattern.

only had the correct proportions but would incorporate some sort of movement similar to that of the naturals.

My first efforts in building a good micro stonefly imitation had several hiccups along the way. The bodies of my initial stones were still too bulky, as even the finest dubbing material just added too much mass. I tried using Microfine and Superfine dubbing, but it just wasn't coming out the way I'd hoped. I even tried using dyed pheasant tail fibers as an alternative for the bodies, but in the end I felt like I was just building another Pheasant Tail variation. I was looking for something entirely different, and I needed the right materials or else it wouldn't be anything new. A thread-bodied version of the Pheasant Tail with influence from a Zebra Midge was what spawned my creation.

One particular winter, conditions were mild, with barely any snowpack and unseasonably warm temperatures. The water temps never dipped below 37 degrees, and the fish in my local tailwater were caught in water types where they typically wouldn't be during that time of year. I had already been doing well on large stonefly imitations, most notably the Shimmer Stone, but I figured this was a good time to try out my smaller stonefly versions once these bugs got active. My efforts went fairly well: I managed to periodically pick off fish from 12 to 18 inches long that day on my slim stonefly imitation. That night I tied a few more of those flies and used cement over the thread body to make it more durable. The head cement worked well and the flies held up better, but after the pattern still wasn't successful enough, I didn't feel like I had devised anything new yet.

A few years later, I stumbled upon a couple new tying materials. Doug Swisher introduced a tying material he called Generation X Wigglies. The material was essentially the finest-diameter silicone/rubber strands on the market. These strands were a fraction of the diameter of standard Spanflex and could easily be used in a smaller pattern. Instantly, I remembered my Winter Stonefly pattern. I ordered a couple of packages of the new material and anxiously awaited their arrival. It was late summer, and I was months away from the time I would be fishing these little stones, but I had to get on the idea while it was fresh in my mind. After I'd ordered the material but before it arrived, I encountered some prolific hatches of little Yellow Sallies while out guiding. Luckily, I had ordered up a whole complement of colors of the Generation X Wigglies, so when they arrived, I was able to try my hand at making a color combo that would closely imitate the nymphal form of those Yellow Sallies.

When my materials came, I found that they would range anywhere from $\frac{1}{2}$ to $1\frac{1}{4}$ inches long and that some of the sections had terrible curves, making them difficult, if not impossible, to work with. To make things easier, I began separating the straighter, usable-size pieces from the smaller, less desirable pieces. I found in time that the longer sections were much easier to tie with and could be cut to length once the fly was completed.

That night I tied up some Infant Stone imitations in shades of bright yellow with a black wire rib and brown with an amber wire rib. The next day I went out on the river in hopes of finding some of the same activity I had experienced the day

Smaller stoneflies are often-overlooked hatches that can occur throughout the season. What they lack in size, they make up for in appeal to trout. JOHN MILLER

prior. As luck would have it, the bugs came off again like clockwork, and they were much heavier this time. Thousands of them were dancing across the water at one point, and I had the perfect testing grounds for the final ingredients in this nearly four-year project.

The afternoon went well. Due to the lower-than-normal flows, I opted to fish a dry-and-dropper rig on 12-foot 5X tapered leader. I started my set up with a size 14 Stimulator with an 8-inch dropper tag of 5X fluorocarbon attached to the eye of the Stimulator. Below that I affixed my new Infant Stone and began casting the rig upstream in the riffles and edges of seams, watching for takes on the Stimulator or any sudden stop, movement, or drop in the water column. For the next couple of hours, I had a blast picking off browns and bows that were gorging on the stonefly nymphs in the riffles. Many of the takes were violent, sinking the Stimulator below the surface or sending it sideways in the drift. To make sure this wasn't some sort of fluke, I fished the stones hard for the next couple of weeks while we still had steady action of little Yellow Sallies. The fly has since proven itself across the country, as well as taking trout frequently on the Beaverhead, Bighorn, Gunnison, Farmington,

Swift, Deerfield, and Westfield Rivers. From other people's accounts, this particular fly works anywhere there are small stoneflies present in the drift.

Fishing

The Infant Stone can be used as a dropper, teamed up in an indicator nymphing system, or used in a Euro nymphing rig as well. Due to the fly's size, it will work best under normal water conditions with fair to excellent clarity. Once you start experiencing heavier flows and diminished clarity, the fly's effectiveness drops, and you're better off with a pattern with a larger profile. I prefer my droppers on smaller patterns a bit longer from time to time, and with these patterns I prefer mine 18 to 24 inches from the lead fly on an indicator rig, and 30 inches apart on any one of the Euro nymphing rigs.

Although this pattern is effective in the heads of pools and riffles and pocketwater, it really shines in those transition zones with moderate and consistent depth and speed. Areas of lower gradient, like glides and runs, are where this fly has been most effective, and although it works well fished under an indicator, it will also work nicely as a dropper below a buoyant dry fly. On rivers with a similar topography, like the upper Delaware watershed, this type of rig works well during periods of smaller stonefly nymph activity or during a hatch. The key to success is figuring out the depth and areas where the fish are holding, then adjusting your droppers accordingly.

Another stealthy technique is to fish a lightly weighted Infant Stone on its own under a coiled sighter, coated with a paste floatant such as Loon Payette Paste or Gink. By floating the coil on the surface and simply retrieving slack as the flies drift downstream, the system works just like an indicator. The coil will unfurl at even a slight strike by a fish. This method usually employs small, light flies and is a refined style of nymphing using leaders anywhere from 15 to 30 or more feet long. This method is best fished on a rod of 10 or 11 feet long in line weights of 2 to 4, with my personal favorites being 10- or 11-foot 3-weight rods. Most casts are directly upstream and typically short, but with some improvisation a cast across and upstream at a 45-degree angle can be fished through a larger expanse of water all the way to a position downstream of the angler. Out of all the Euro nymphing styles of fishing, the French style is my favorite, as it is a fast-paced, constant-action method when employed properly.

You can attach the sighter to a leader of any length you desire. I suggest something a bit shorter than 30 feet and typically go with a 15- to 18-foot tapered leader in 0X to 2X to aid in casting. From the sighter, I will attach my tippet to my single small Infant Stone, which is usually lightly weighted with either a 1.5-, 2.0-, or 2.4-millimeter bead. Anything heavier will sink the coiled sighter. The idea is to have the sighter floating on the surface of the water as you cast directly upstream. The most important factor is choosing a section of tippet that will be slightly longer or shallower than the average water depth, so you can suspend the fly from the bottom of the stream as it drifts toward you. Sometimes, a longer section of tippet is better, as

the fish may be near the bottom. This will require a little guesswork on your part, but this can be a deadly method by which to fish this particular fly. Over the course of the last few seasons, this particular method has worked well especially in slower water presentations or when the water is below normal flows. The technique itself is stealthy and gives the angler an advantage for a variety of reasons, most importantly a downstream position and a long leader.

Variations

Over time, I found a few materials, old and new, that have made this pattern easier to construct. The first of which was a longer hanked version of the the micro diameter rubber or Swisher's Generation X Wigglies that I mentioned. Hareline Dubbin introduced a material called Daddy Long Legs. It's the exact same material as Senyo's Shaggy Dub and the Wigglies, only it is left approximately 8 inches long and comes in a hank wrapped with a zip tie. What I liked about this material is that I no longer had to sort through the different lengths in a bag, and I could now leave the legs long when I tied them to the shank, then trim them after, making them easier to work with.

Over time I did away with wing cases cut from Thin Skin or strands of pearlescent flashy material. I really like the look of flat Diamond Braid, but due to its size I couldn't substitute it into my pattern until Hareline Dubbin introduced the Midge Diamond Braid. Midge Diamond Braid is a scaled down version of the standard Diamond Braid. The smaller size ended up being the perfect match for the Infant Stone. This material isn't overly flashy, adding just the right amount of subtle flash to the pattern, and it's extremely durable. Now, instead of coating the thread bodies and wing cases with head cement, I use Clear Cure Goo Hydro, as it cures almost instantly, doesn't discolor, and makes the flies virtually bombproof.

Lastly, the easiest and most effective way to add a little weight to the Infant Stone is by changing the type of bead you use. If I need something to sink quickly, then I use tungsten beads in 1.5-, 2.0-, or 2.4-millimeter sizes. If getting them down in the water column quickly isn't that much of a concern, then I stick with the standard brass beads.

BROWN INFANT STONE

Hook: #12-16 Partridge Sproat Wet
Bead: Copper tungsten (1.5–2.5 mm)
Thread: Rusty brown 70-denier Ultra Thread
Appendages: Brown Hareline Daddy Long Legs
Abdomen: Tying thread
Rib: Amber Ultra Wire (small)
Thorax: Brown mole fur or Hareline Microfine Dubbing
Wing Case: Black Hareline Midge Diamond Braid

Note: You can substitute a #14-20 Tiemco 100 for the hook.

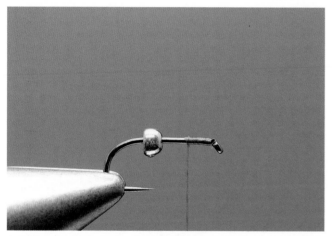

1. Slide a bead on the hook, then affix the hook in the vise. Slide the bead rearward toward the bend of the hook, and attach your tying thread directly behind the hook eye. To ensure this step goes smoothly, always use 70-denier thread, as it will build less bulk in the fly.

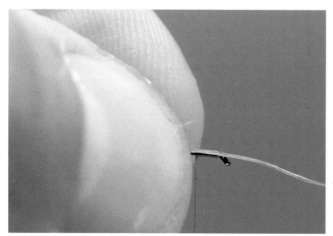

2. Tie a 2- to 3-inch long Daddy Long Leg to the top of the hook shank with four or five thread wraps working back toward the hook eye.

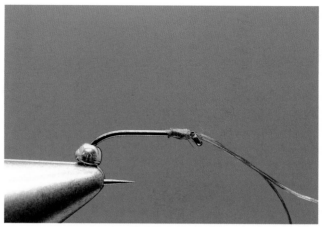

3. Fold the other section of the Daddy Long Leg forward over the hook eye, and wrap your tying thread rearward to the end of the thread wraps using more tension. This will ensure that the thread will compress the rubber antennae using minimal amounts of thread. Whip-finish and clip the thread.

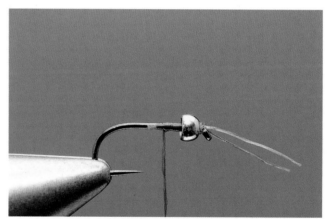

4. Slide the bead back forward over the thread wraps, seating it firmly to the front of the hook, and reattach the tying thread behind the bead and cover a third of the hook shank with thread. Trim the antennae to length, roughly the length of the hook or slightly longer.

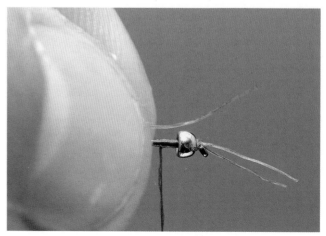

5. Tie another pair of 2- to 3-inch Daddy Long Leg in on top of the hook with two or three turns of thread.

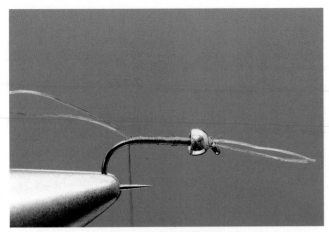

6. Fold the forward-facing section of Daddy Long Leg rearward while maintaining tension on the thread. Continue wrapping the thread over the two sections until you reach the point where the hook bend starts making your final wrap of thread underneath the tail, propping it up off the fly.

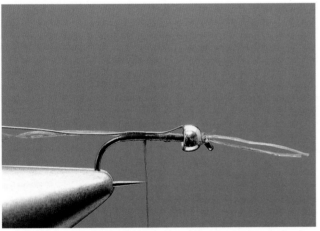

7. Tie in the wire rib on the top side of the hook shank keeping constant pressure on the thread so as not to roll the wire around the hook.

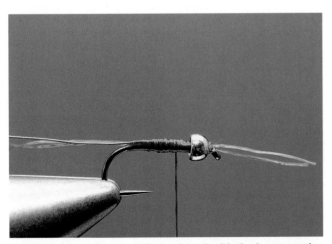

8. Build a tapered cone with the thread with the larger portion closer to the bead.

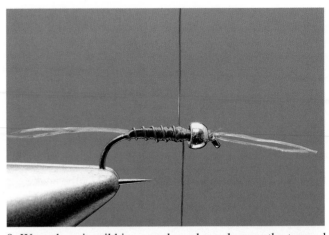

9. Wrap the wire ribbing openly and evenly over the tapered thread body. Continue wrapping past the midway point, as we will add our wing case in a subsequent step and want to make sure we secure the ribbing well.

10. To ensure durability, add a thin layer of head cement or Clear Cure Goo Hydro to the abdomen.

11. Tie in a wing case on the top of the hook shank making sure that the wing case is close to the front third of the fly.

12. Tie in a pair of Daddy Long Legs on the top of the hook with two loose wraps. Pull one pair to the near side and the other to the far side of the hook, and then cover with six to eight wraps of thread to form a pair of X-shaped legs on either side of the body.

13. Dub a uniform noodle of Microfine Dubbing to the thread, and wrap the noodle over the thread wraps.

14. Pull the Midge Diamond Braid over the top of the fly, and secure it with thread three to four wraps behind and in front of the material. Whip-finish and trim your tying thread. To ensure added durability, add a drop of head cement or Clear Cure Goo Hydro to the wing case and thread collar. Trim the legs and tail so that they are roughly the same length as the antenna.

15. Notice the relatively fine diameter of the appendages and natural taper of the thread-based abdomen.

BLACK INFANT STONE

YELLOW/GOLDEN INFANT STONE

Hook:	#12-16 Partridge Sproat Wet
Bead:	Black tungsten (1.5–2.5 mm)
Thread:	Black 70- or 140-denier Ultra Thread
Appendages:	Black Hareline Daddy Long Legs
Abdomen:	Tying thread
Rib:	Silver Ultra Wire (small)
Thorax:	Black mole fur or Hareline Microfine Dubbing
Wing Case:	Black Hareline Midge Diamond Braid

Note: You can substitute a #14-20 Tiemco 100 for the hook.

Hook:	#12-16 Partridge Sproat Wet
Bead:	Gold tungsten (1.5–2.5 mm)
Thread:	Yellow 70- or 140-denier Ultra Thread
Appendages:	Yellow Hareline Daddy Long Legs
Abdomen:	Tying thread
Rib:	Black Ultra Wire (small)
Thorax:	Sulphur yellow Hareline Microfine Dubbing
Wing Case:	Black Hareline Midge Diamond Braid

Note: You can substitute a #14-20 Tiemco 100 for the hook.

CHAPTER 11

Classified Caddis Pupa

During a caddis emergence, trout will key in on the pupae as they ascend the water column and feed with reckless abandon. I've been on the water when the sun is high during one of these events, and I've watched the trouts' flanks glistening in the water column as they slash at the pupae. If you're fortunate enough to see this, and to have the right color and size pupa pattern, the fishing can be red hot.

The late Gary LaFontaine opened the fly-fishing world's eyes to the importance of caddisflies to trout. He devised the Sparkle Pupa and Deep Sparkle Pupa, which are two of the most effective and innovative caddis pupa patterns to date. Using Antron, an air-capturing synthetic fiber, gives the fly a lifelike appearance reminiscent of the natural as it captures air

Caddis pupae imitations do not necessarily have to be exact. Often, suggestive imitations will do the trick, as is the case with the Classified Caddis Pupa.

and ascends through the water column. These two patterns are my all-time favorite designs by LaFontaine, and as a younger tier, they gave me fits when I tried to replicate them. Although I could roughly mimic the perfectly proportioned bubbled Antron bodies on occasion, I was never satisfied with my overall efforts.

When I was just tying for myself, I could endure the time it took to painstakingly construct these flies, and in time I got proficient with it. Once I began guiding, I constantly struggled with tying these flies, and strived for something less time-consuming. My first attempts were futile, and the patterns weren't as effective as LaFontaine's.

Frustration settled in for a couple of seasons. Through the season, the rivers I guided on had excellent caddis activity, and to keep my clients with bent rods and smiles, I found myself replenishing my stocks after every trip. I needed to find a better method soon, as I was spending too much time every night on the vise putting those bugs together.

It just so happened a close friend of mine introduced me to an interesting material that would fix my problems. My good friend and fishing best buddy Mike and I were talking on the phone one day while he was still out West on the Bighorn Reservation. Somehow we got on the subject of the Sparkle Pupa and using Antron fibers in the construction of the fly. Mike mentioned how he fished a scud pattern that was devised by a guide on the Bighorn that used chopped Antron fibers from a carpet spun in a dubbing brush for the body. That spring Mike and I were fishing the Bighorn together using that exact scud and I learned firsthand how effective it was.

The scud pattern in question was a simple tie. The original pattern was constructed out of tying thread and a loop of black or red holographic flash with the Antron carpet fibers sandwiched in between and spun in a brush. After that, you wound the brush forward in open wraps toward the eye of the hook, tied off, and then brushed the fibers downward toward the hook point, imitating the legs and trimmed flush across the back or top of the hook shank. Mike and I substituted the holographic

Close-up photograph of a wet, recently fished tan Classified Caddis Pupa. Notice that when wet, the body changes the entire profile of the fly so that it's similar to a natural caddis pupa.

flash with Brassie size Ultra Wire for durability on the patterns we tied for ourselves, and they fished just as good as the original design. While we were floating down the river that day, I asked Mike if he recalled how many colors of the dubbing material were available, and if they had any insect-related colors on the market. Mike was pretty certain that they did, and he reminded me that Yellowstone Fly Goods based out of Montana sold the dubbing.

When we got home from our trip to the Bighorn, I immediately purchased every color of dubbing. Looking at the initial stocks of Scud Dub that I had purchased, I didn't like the colors they offered in shades of green. They were either too muted or way too bright to match what I had in mind to imitate the Grannom pupae I encountered on my home waters. The chartreuse Scud Dub was the closest thing to what I was looking for, but it was a little too yellow in my book. I had to improvise, but how? One day while tinkering with this pattern, I thought, why not try using an alternative colored wire to achieve the effect I was looking for? I remembered this technique from discussions that I had with Dave Goulet, owner of Classic & Custom Fly Shop. Dave frequently used different colors of thread with some of the dubbing blends he used on his dry flies and nymphs to achieve colors that looked like the natural. At the time, a spool of green Ultra Wire was staring me right in the face. You could speculate it was fate, or coincidence, or maybe I'm just reading into it a bit too much. At the end of it all I had a nice dubbing brush with a darker spine as a result of the green Ultra Wire, and even without it being wet, I had a feeling this could be something.

Like many of the nymphs that I have concocted, the concept for this pattern was already in my mind. After twisting up a couple of dubbing brushes, I immediately began constructing the pattern. Now I build all of my brushes ahead of time and then begin the tying process. Because of the variety

A close up photograph of a caddis pupa. Notice the bulbous shape and wingpads across the top. JOHN MILLER

CHAPTER 12

Rock Candy Larva

Most of the rivers in the Northeastern United States have healthy populations of caddis, and throughout the season I take trout on imitations of their larval form. Most caddis larva patterns are fairly simple to tie and require only a few materials to construct. Often, when kicked loose in the drift, a caddis larva will curl, which makes it an excellent candidate for being tied on scud or grub hooks.

Caddis larvae are some of the most prevalent species that inhabit fast, well-oxygenated stretches of most trout streams, and for this reason, you can imitate them with fast sinking, heavy flies—the kind common in the tight-line styles of fishing that have grown more popular in the United States over the last decade. This European-style nymphing, as it is often called,

Caddis larvae come in a variety of colors and sizes. With a few minor changes, the Rock Candy Larva can imitate any specific caddis larva you may encounter.

works best in turbulent, varied water, with depths less than 3 feet. In order to penetrate this type of water and get your flies into the zone quickly, you often need nymphs in a variety of sizes and weights. These are commonly called "anchor" flies because they anchor the team of flies in the water column as a result of their weight and drastically aid in the detection of strikes.

Because these nymphs have extra weight, they will snag from time to time even though they're constructed to ride inverted. The risk of losing them is fairly high, so I favor patterns I can tie quickly. If the fly takes more than three minutes to tie, then I probably don't want to incorporate it in my weighted nymph selection. There are exceptions, but generally speaking, three minutes is my limit.

The Rock Candy Larva evolved from a general caddis larva imitation that worked for me under a wide array of conditions. The Jelly Rope Caddis is about as simple a caddis larva pattern as it gets: hook, bead, Jelly Rope–wrapped body, and a collar of coarse dubbing complete the recipe. With practice, just about anyone can tie this fly in a minute or two, which makes it perfect for an anchor with some additional weight. The body of the fly has fantastic segmentation as a result of the Jelly

Rope, and with some alterations in color, you can replicate a vast array of caddis.

The only downfall with Jelly Rope is that it is a solid, rubber like material that has minimal elasticity and a limited ability to compress even when tied under heavy thread tension. When tying with Jelly Rope, you need to cut it at an angle so that it can be affixed to the hook without slipping. If the angle of cut is too steep, no matter how much thread tension you place on the Jelly Rope, it will still result in a misshapen body with a bump near the tail of the fly.

Due to this problem, the Jelly Rope Caddis isn't a prime candidate for an anchor. Because Jelly Rope does not compress, when adding several turns of lead or lead-free wire in the underbody of the fly, the overall proportions of the pattern change drastically. The completed fly will look more like an overinflated tire than a caddis larva. My attempts at building a fly similar in nature just never quite worked out, forcing me to forget the idea for a while.

I don't remember the exact day it hit me, but in the midst of a busy spring filled with frantically tying guide flies and ordering copious amounts of materials to do so, I received a

Michael Schmidt high-sticks a section of pocketwater on the Farmington River. Caddis larvae typically inhabit fast, well-oxygenated sections of river, and trout will readily fall for a caddis larva imitation in these waters.

Caddis larvae come in a variety of colors and sizes and inhabit faster water, making them readily available to trout since they often become loose in the drift. JOHN MILLER

Uni-Stretch is a great alternative for building underbodies without using excessive amounts of thread. The late Dick Talleur introduced the fly-tying world to the many uses of this material well over a decade ago.

sample package of Flat Body Glass, a product by the European company Sybai. While ordering several packages of tungsten beads, flat lead, and a variety of other materials that were rare in America at the time, my friend Kevin Compton of Performance Flies had slipped in a package or two of this interesting product with my order.

My curiosity got the best of me, and I tore into the package immediately. What I found inside was a flat, translucent, rub-

bery material that was approximately $1/4$ inch wide and thin, unlike the Jelly Rope that I was accustomed to. I could stretch this material to twice its length in my hand, and when I let go, it would rebound back to its original size. In other words, this product had tremendous elasticity, and the coloring was uniform so that as it stretched it did not change.

I had a spool of 140 Ultra Thread in fluorescent chartreuse on a bobbin lying on the desk, and another spool of green Uni-Stretch sitting next to it, possibly because I was tying caddis larvae that week. The most effective colors of caddis larvae patterns from my experience have been shades of green to olive, so I figured I would start from there. At the time, I was also successful with patterns that had hot spot collars, and fluorescent chartreuse was by default the hot spot of choice when I tied larval patterns in those shades of green.

What happened next was a stroke of luck, and I later determined that this may well be the trigger in this pattern's effectiveness. After laying a foundation of flat lead wire and doubling it back to the midpoint of the fly, I covered the lead quickly and evenly with the green Uni-Stretch to ensure that I had a nice smooth taper to the underbody. Rather than change the tying thread to a similar shade of green, my laziness reared its ugly head, and I just grabbed the bobbin already spooled up with the fluorescent chartreuse 140-denier Ultra Thread and affixed it behind the tungsten bead of the fly. After half a dozen turns, I spiraled the Ultra Thread down to the rear of the fly quickly instead of covering the Uni-Stretch in its entirety as usual.

Once I got to the rear of the fly, I took a section of the green body glass, cut the end at a 45-degree angle and caught the point of it with my tying thread. As I stretched the body glass, overlapping the material by 50 percent on each turn, I also loosened the tension on the material so that it would make the segmentation more pronounced as it closed in on the head of the fly.

Once I tied off the body glass, I made a collar of dubbing for the legs directly behind the bead. I finished the fly off with a double five-turn whip-finish to make a pronounced hot spot collar of thread, and added some head cement.

This particular fly was quick and easy, and I whipped up a dozen or so for my next outing, taking maybe twenty minutes to do so. I was having great success at the time with bright green rock worm imitations, so I made sure that I tied up a healthy stash of these in green with black beads and black collars of dubbing. That next morning I headed out earlier than my scheduled guide trip and put the fly through the paces.

The pattern was durable—so durable that to this day the finish will wear off the tungsten bead before the body glass will separate from the fly. And now, instead of head cement, I use Clear Cure Goo Hydro in the construction of the fly, making it even more durable.

Fishing

As expected, the Rock Candy didn't disappoint on its maiden voyage. We brought several fish to hand in an hour, and a couple of hefty 18- to 20-inch browns. My client that day tested the pattern as well; in fact, we never changed our anchors that day. What we learned on that first outing was due to the elasticity of the body glass, the fly would roll and bounce along the bottom like a Super Ball, resulting in few if any hang ups. We could free most of the snags we encountered by quickly changing our position or changing the angle of the rod.

Fished on a tight line through water a few inches deep up to 4 or 5 feet, in a fast to moderately fast current, this fly excelled. The Rock Candy Larva has become the fly I turn to most when I need an anchor fly to penetrate through fast water with minimal hangups. The depth and the speed of the water will dictate how large and heavy of a fly I use, but I find that I can cover most situations with a size 10 or a 12 with a $1/8$- to $5/32$-inch tungsten bead and $1 1/2$ layers of flat lead. If I need more weight, I can either fish a pair in tandem, add more shot to the line, or increase the size to 6 or 8 with more weight and $3/16$-inch tungsten beads.

Over the last few seasons, I've found that prior to or during a caddisfly emergence, this fly works well imitating the drifting larvae. Due to the fly's ability to excel in fast water, I'm fairly certain that it's taken as a pupa as well, and so I often will accentuate a swing in my presentation at the end of my drift. This leads to aggressive strikes that I can feel easily as long as I'm in contact with the flies throughout the course of the drift.

I've also had success with the Rock Candy Larva early in the morning, and I presume that this is due mostly in part to the fact that caddis larvae in general are known to experience behavioral drift earlier in the day, or a repositioning of themselves in a watershed for a variety of reasons. Caddis larvae are

Tying a bunch of Rock Candy is simple and quick. A pile of this size is more than enough for a couple seasons worth of fishing.

Once I find a pattern that works, I like to have a good assortment on hand. The Rock Candy Larva is super durable and will outlast the finish on the bead, as is evident by the brown chipped bead on the far right of the second row up from the bottom. That particular fly had caught dozens of fish.

a great choice to imitate under a wide variety of circumstances, especially when you're searching new waters for the first time, as caddis are abundant in many streams that hold trout, the trout readily recognize them as a food source.

Where you place the fly in your team of flies can also make a difference in your level of success. Typically, once you figure out where the fish are feeding in the water column, you can adjust the position of your anchor in your team. I will often start with my Rock Candy Larva on point, meaning the bottom position. If I keep catching fish on the pattern in that position, then I can be fairly certain that the fish are opportunistic feeders, predominantly closer to the stream bed. If I have marginal success on the pattern in that position, then I may move it to one of the dropper tags. This is often the best position during an emergence, as the fish may be feeding in various levels of the water column. Nothing beats experimentation, so be willing to mix up your flies position often until you find just where the fish are feeding.

I later learned a little trick to avoid having to change my fly when the paint chips off the bead from contact with the bottom. You can color the exposed metal with a permanent marker and then coat the marker with UV resin and cure it with the rays from sun or a small battery-operated UV torch. Now, I keep a black Sharpie marker and UV Knot Sense by Loon in my pack to quickly do some streamside repair to the chipped beads. In a pinch it works wonders, especially if your supply of flies is limited for that day. Be sure to dry that fly off as much as you can before coloring the bead with the marker, as it will not adhere to the bare metal when wet.

Variations

The Rock Candy Larva has become my top caddis larva pattern and anchor for all the reasons I touched upon earlier. I have yet to find a larva that equals its durability, tying simplicity, and ability to catch fish. Those three traits combined are what set this fly apart from other imitations, as I can whip up a couple dozen of them in under an hour, and be off to the river fishing.

Over the course of a few seasons, and from prior experience, I found it doesn't hurt to have a variety of other colors in your fly arsenal, as caddis larvae are not just shades of green or olive. Caddis are diverse and come in a wide range of colors. Sometimes, the same species of caddis may be a completely different shade or color altogether from watershed to watershed, or even in different stretches of the same watershed. This is due largely to the makeup of the stream. For example, many of the free-living caddis I find on my home waters vary tremendously in color based upon their location.

What I have found is that my favorite colors and sizes for the various sections of the river are different, so I've concluded that a wide spectrum of sizes and colors is far more beneficial than having several of the same color in just a couple of sizes. Do a kick sample on your home waters, look at the colors of the caddis larvae you find, and try to replicate them. Body glass comes in dozens of colors, so there's a good chance you can find the color you need.

To create a darker back, you can color the topside of the underbody with a permanent marker in the color of your choice. You can also use a permanent marker to color one edge of the body glass prior to wrapping the body if you want to get a defined, segmented look. This is a technique borrowed from Oliver Edwards, and it is a quick fix if you are looking for a more segmented larva.

One other little trick I have done is tie in a section of flash material and secure it over the topside of the underbody prior to wrapping the body glass. Put a small drop of superglue or Zap-A-Gap on the top before pulling your flash material over the top to prevent it from rolling around to the side of the fly. Once you let the glue cure for a few seconds, you can tie down the material and then wrap your body glass.

BRIGHT GREEN ROCK CANDY LARVA (Black Bead Version)	
Hook:	#6-14 Tiemco 2499 SPBL
Bead:	Black tungsten, size to match
Underbody:	Flat lead wire covered with green Uni-Stretch
Thread:	Fluorescent chartreuse 140-denier Ultra Thread
Body:	Green Sybai Flat Body Glass
Legs:	Black Spiky Squirrel or Hareline Dubbin
Hot Spot:	Fluorescent chartreuse 140-denier Ultra Thread or chartreuse Datum Glo-Bright

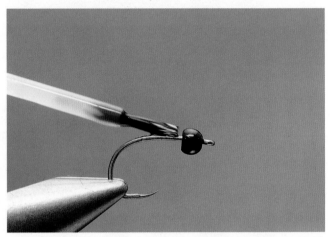

1. Slide a tungsten bead onto the hook and seat it at the hook eye. Apply a thin drop of superglue on the hook shank behind the bead.

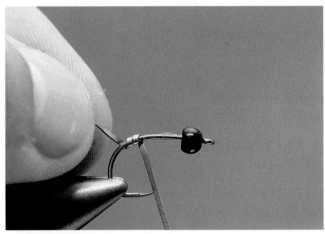

2. Begin wrapping a section of medium-diameter flat lead wire around the hook in consecutive wraps, starting from a point at the beginning of hook bend.

3. Pinch the rear section of lead wire off with your thumb nail, then continue wrapping the wire forward, seating the wire against the bead.

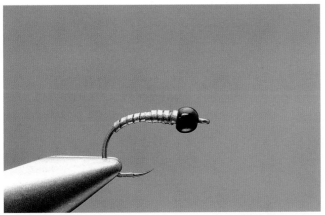

4. Reverse the wire rearward and take three or four more turns over the top of the first layer of wire, then break it free using your thumb nail. This will aid in building a quick taper to the body of the fly.

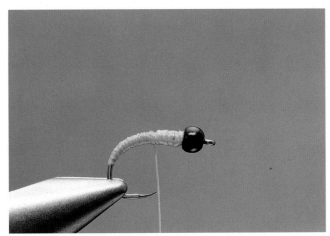

5. Attach the Uni-Stretch behind the bead and work a base covering the lead underbody to a point at the halfway point of the hook bend. Run the Uni-Stretch back toward the bead, building an even progressive cone toward the bead, then whip-finish and cut the Uni-Stretch.

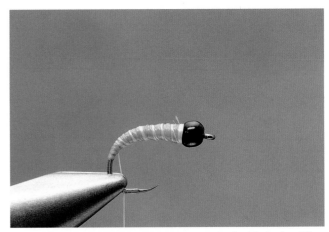

6. Replace the Uni-Stretch with a spool of 140-denier Ultra Thread, and attach it with four to six wraps behind the bead, and then half hitch the thread. Begin spiral-wrapping the thread to a point approximately a bead's length back from the rear of the underbody.

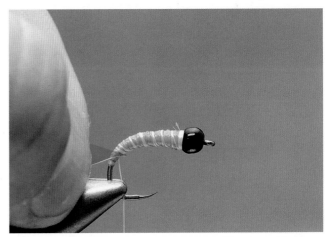

7. Cut the end of a section of Flat Body Glass at a 45-degree angle. Take the section of Body Glass flat side up, and catch the tip of the material with your tying thread.

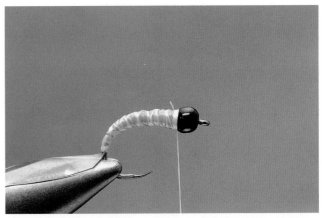

8. Continue securing the Body Glass to the rear of the hook with five or six turns of thread, being sure to cover the underbody. Once you have securely wrapped the Body Glass, spiral-wrap the thread back directly behind the bead.

9. Begin wrapping the Body Glass forward toward the bead of the hook. Be sure to stretch the material as you wrap it, while also overlapping each wrap 50 percent. This will create a neatly segmented body.

10. Tie off the Body Glass with three or four turns of thread behind and in front of the Body Glass. Half hitch and then cover up the ends with a few more thread wraps, creating a neat thread collar behind the bead. Half hitch your thread.

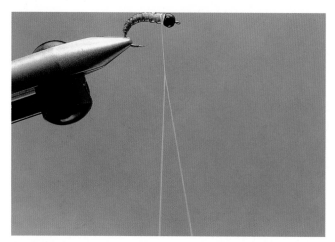

11. Split the thread in half with the tip of scissors to make an open loop.

12. Grab a small clump, roughly an inch or two long of Spiky Squirrel or Hareline Dubbin, tie it in between the two sections of split thread, and close the thread around the dubbing clump.

13. Twist the thread and run your finger and thumb upward toward the dubbing rope. This will close the thread around the dubbing mass like a dubbing brush. This also allows the dubbing to take on a coarser appearance. Once you have secured the loop, begin wrapping the noodle over the thread wraps behind the bead to create the collar.

14. After wrapping the collar, begin building a hot spot collar out of the thread directly between the bead and dubbing collar. This will force the dubbing fibers back over the rear portion of the fly. Whip-finish and cement the thread wraps for durability.

When you turn on a UV light above the fly, notice how the fluorescent thread lights up, creating a multi-segmented fly.

BRIGHT GREEN ROCK CANDY LARVA
(Copper Bead Version)

Hook:	#6-14 Tiemco 2499 SPBL
Bead:	Copper tungsten, size to match
Underbody:	Flat lead wire covered with green Uni-Stretch
Thread:	Fluorescent chartreuse 140-denier Ultra Thread
Body:	Green Sybai Flat Body Glass
Legs:	Brown Spiky Squirrel or Hareline Dubbin
Hot Spot:	Fluorescent chartreuse 140-denier Ultra Thread or chartreuse Datum Glo-Bright

OLIVE ROCK CANDY LARVA
(Copper Bead Version)

Hook:	#6-14 Tiemco 2499 SPBL
Bead:	Copper tungsten, size to match
Underbody:	Flat lead wire covered with olive Uni-Stretch
Thread:	Olive 140-denier Ultra Thread
Body:	Olive Sybai Flat Body Glass
Legs:	Brown Spiky Squirrel or Hareline Dubbin
Hot Spot:	Fluorescent chartreuse 140-denier Ultra Thread or chartreuse Datum Glo-Bright

OLIVE ROCK CANDY LARVA
(Black Bead Version)

Hook:	#6-14 Tiemco 2499 SPBL
Bead:	Black tungsten, size to match
Underbody:	Flat lead wire covered with olive Uni-Stretch
Thread:	Olive 140-denier Ultra Thread
Body:	Olive Sybai Flat Body Glass
Legs:	Black Spiky Squirrel or Hareline Dubbin
Hot Spot:	Fluorescent chartreuse 140-denier Ultra Thread or chartreuse Datum Glo-Bright

HONEY ROCK CANDY LARVA

Hook:	#6-14 Tiemco 2499 SPBL
Bead:	Brown tungsten, size to match
Underbody:	Flat lead wire covered with white Uni-Stretch
Thread:	Cream 140-denier Ultra Thread
Body:	Honey Sybai Flat Body Glass
Legs:	Black Spiky Squirrel or Hareline Dubbin
Hot Spot:	Fluorescent yellow Datum Glo-Bright

CHAPTER 13

Woven Mayfly

When the Euro nymphing craze struck the United States several years ago, I was fascinated with a variety of the fly patterns devised by competitive anglers across the globe. Many of us in the States had huge misconceptions about fly design and Euro nymphing. One of the most prevalent was that Euro nymphing was nothing more than a style of nymph fishing hinged around heavily weighted flies on a short line. Many soon found out that this was merely one of the many styles used.

The beauty of several of the short-line techniques was they excelled in fast, riffled or pocket-strewn water where the fish have to make quick decisions about what to eat. This type of water can be a pleasure to fish, as the trout have little time to inspect your fly. If it generally resembles some of the common

Many mayfly nymphs have broad-shaped bodies with distinct color variations from top to bottom. The Woven Mayfly Nymph is my attempt at loosely mimicking these characteristics.

food forms, it will get eaten. You may have noticed that many of the patterns are simple, relatively easy to tie, with general patterns for smaller mayflies or caddis, for example. To round out my pattern selection, I was looking to design a general nymph pattern that could easily be taken for a mayfly or stonefly nymph and was moderately weighted but had a distinct difference in color from top to bottom. This pattern had to be versatile enough that it could be fished in both a long- or short-line Euro nymphing system.

I had also been experimenting with different ways to make two-toned nymphs. Most mayfly and stonefly nymphs have dis-

DMC Embroidery yarn is a six-strand yarn that comes in 8 meter reams for a dollar. It can be found at any craft store and comes in hundreds of colors.

To make the tying process with woven flies go smoother, I like to wind it on an empty thread spool and use a bobbin to control it. The spool on the left consists of a full six-strand yarn, and the spool on the bobbin is separated to two-strand. You may find that two- or three-strand is better for smaller nymphs in the size 10 to 16 range, and more strands for larger.

tinct changes in color from top to bottom. Typically, most nymphs have darker backs and lighter undersides. The back of a nymph on many rivers will take on the color of the stream bottom. For years I tinkered with two-toned nymphs, as I had watched on numerous occasions the naturals drifting in the water column. As the nymphs drifted, they would flip and turn, and you could easily see their lighter colored underbellies. I often thought this could be a trigger built into a fly. In my experience, using different colors is one of the most overlooked triggers in nymph pattern design. Flashy colored wing cases, shellbacks, and ribs imitated this natural appearance well, and I felt that if I could accurately imitate this feature, I could build a pattern that was a little different from the rest.

One of the most notable fly patterns that came from Euro nymphing is the Polish Woven Nymph, a general attractor pattern that uses a technique called the shuttle weave to make a two-toned woven bodied fly. The fly itself is basic; the abdomen region of the fly is woven with a collar of dubbing and a rib. The pattern's general design suggests a variety of potential trout food. I had seen woven flies before, most notably George Grant's Woven Stone, which I was fond of, and I thought I could incorporate the woven body into a more realistic mayfly imitation.

My revelation came just before the first major mayfly hatch we experience here in the Northeast. The Hendrickson Mayfly (*Ephemerella subvaria*) nymphs are stout and come from the family of crawlers. They range anywhere from size 10 to 14 and are an important nymph to trout. The Hendrickson nymph has a distinctly lighter colored underbody, and its stout body can easily be imitated with a weighted underbody without throwing off the proportions of the pattern. Most of the woven patterns that were popular among fishermen at the time used a technique called the shuttle weave. The shuttle weave is a fairly easy technique to learn, but it requires a little bit of practice to get the hang of. A pair of bobbins can make the technique easy to master as they will allow you to control the amount of tension needed to construct the weave correctly.

You can use a variety of materials to construct the woven body section of the fly, but probably the easiest one is embroidery floss. DMC embroidery floss is a six-strand cotton floss that comes in over 450 colors and is readily available at your local craft store. Depending on the size of the fly that you're going to weave, you can separate the strands into the number that is most conducive for the fly you are trying to construct. Typically, I have found that two or three strands work best on most nymphs in sizes 6 to 16. You can easily tie dozens and dozens of flies from one skein if you separate the floss into two-strand sections.

A good friend I met through fly fishing, Jerry Jahn, turned me on to an easy way to tie woven bodies. I was talking with Jerry one day in the local fly shop and expressed my disgust with the tediousness of tying woven flies. Jerry being a commercial tier, and a talented one I might add, offered some sound tips on tying these flies. He instructed me to wind each parcel of floss onto an empty thread spool. Once on the spool, the embroidery floss could then be affixed to a tying bobbin, which made tying and thread control a much easier and more efficient task. It was one of those gee-why-didn't-I-think-of-that moments for me, but

Coq de Leon feathers are excellent choices for tailing materials on many dries and nymphs that require a little more rigid material. They are naturally barred and long enough to tail virtually any insect imitation.

it was one that shortened the learning curve tremendously while also cutting my tying time down significantly.

For the tails on this particular pattern, I resorted to a feather not readily used in the states for nymphs. The late Dick Talleur introduced me to Coq de Leon feathers when he visited my local fishing club many, many years ago. What I loved about Coq de Leon was it had even barring across the barbs and was fairly long and stiff, making it ideal tailing material for dry flies and some nymphs that had rigid tails. A small patch of Coq de Leon will tail hundreds of flies, and the size range is dynamic, allowing the tier to use the material in a wide spectrum of fly sizes.

After spinning up roughly a dozen or more of these new nymphs in a size 12, half moderately weighted with $1/8$-inch tungsten beads, and the other half with $5/32$-inch tungsten beads, I waited for the right time to try these flies out. The third week of April is usually when we see the Hendrickson hatch in my neck of the woods, but weather and water conditions can affect the timing of this hatch. Emergence is usually in the early afternoon, with spinner falls in the evening after the first week of heavy hatch activity. In the hours before the hatch, usually mid to late morning, the nymphs will become active and the fish take note, often sliding into the heads of pools and riffles to pick off these large meals.

Water conditions and weather found us fishing the hatch the first week of April, as we had experienced a mild winter and the spring temperatures were above the seasonal norms, moving everything forward by a few weeks. The only downfall to fishing this particular hatch on my home water is it really draws a crowd. Most of the fishermen know that the Hendrickson hatch can bring up some of the largest fish in the stream to the surface to feed, so many anglers will often plan vacation time around this event. You may find that your favorite piece of water is now occupied by several other anglers. Residing close to the river and being on the water often as a guide, I usually got the

luxury of timing the hatches knowing where they would be in the watershed.

I stepped into one of my favorite riffles in the middle of the trout management area on the Farmington and tied the heavier of the two new nymphs on point with a darker colored Hare's Ear for a dropper. I figured I better have one of the old standbys on there to gauge the effectiveness of this pattern. The results were noteworthy: The Woven Mayfly on this day steadily yielded fish in the faster water at the heads of the pools, holding its own with the Hare's Ear. What I found was that once I started working my way into the belly or gut of the run below the riffles, the Hare's Ear would catch more fish. I spent the better part of that day intentionally fishing the pair of flies through all sorts of water types, and the same held true for the duration of my outing.

That particular season I tied the Woven Mayfly in a variety of color schemes to cover the spectrum of medium to larger mayfly and stonefly nymphs and had good success with them in diverse conditions. What I also found was I could really fine-tune how heavy I made the fly by the type of bead and underbody I used. If I needed a transitional pattern that was moderately weighted and could be used in an indicator rig, I would use a brass bead and lead-free wire in the underbody. This particular pattern in larger sizes proved to be a successful pattern under high and dirty conditions. A large size 4 to 6 Woven Mayfly in shades of olive and orange, brown and yellow, and black and yellow is a great searching pattern when the rivers are swollen. Trout easily recognize the larger profile under those conditions, and this pattern has proven effective when fished in the shallow margins and edges of the stream close to the banks.

Fishing

In short time I recognized that this pattern was yet another versatile nymph that could be fished in a variety of disciplines. My thoughts were to fish this pattern in a shorter Czech or Polish nymph system, but I quickly found that a moderately weighted Woven Mayfly can work well as an anchor in the longer line French and Spanish nymphing systems. What I like about the French and the Spanish systems is although they require a little more dexterity and skill to employ, they allow the angler to fish through water that is a little farther away from the angler. Distance between you and your target is often a good thing regardless of what water type you are fishing, as it will cut down on the number of fish you alert to your presence. Also, the waters that I frequent are excellent examples of fisheries where these techniques are effective. Shallow riffles, pockets, and glides that are best approached and fished from downstream are ideal for these two methods, and this particular pattern in the right weights can be deadly.

The March Brown nymph, for example, migrates from midstream to the edges of streams when it is ready to hatch. Because the nymphs are a large meal, anywhere from a size 10 to as big as a 6 in some rare cases, trout often move to these areas when the nymphs are active. Some large trout will set up in shallow feeding lanes off the banks to intercept these nymphs.

If I could only tie one color of this fly, I'd tie the brown and yellow version. I typically tie a dozen in sizes 8 to 12 every year as they are some of the most dependable sizes.

Many mayfly nymphs have distinct color differences from top to bottom. A nymph imitation that replicates these attributes will at times be more effective than single-color patterns. JOHN MILLER

Many times during periods of March Brown activity, my clients and I have taken some real bruisers in the shallow margins tight to shore. Be sure to have a wide variety of weights in these patterns so that you can easily adjust for different conditions.

Some species of stoneflies do the same thing, like the Western Salmonfly for example. Although I had devised this pattern specifically to be fished in a tight-line Euro nymphing rig, I quickly realized the pattern could be successfully fished under an indicator or beneath a large buoyant dry fly in a dry-and-dropper rig. My only suggestion if you plan on tying some for these rigs is to go lighter on the lead underbody or the bead head. Often, if you just substitute the tungsten bead with a brass bead and use lead or lead-free wire in the underbody, the fly will sink plenty. If you tie them with too much weight, they will sink even the most buoyant pattern, so adjust accordingly.

To keep the weights separated for the same patterns, put them in different sections of your fly box and use different-colored thread collars as a means to color code them. A few of the competition anglers that I've spoken with use that trick often. I've seen the fly boxes of many competitive anglers, and many are precise on the exact weight of the flies, often weighing them on a gram scale and color coding their entire fly selections. Although I admire the level of precision, I am a little more rudimentary and will tie several of the same pattern with different-size tungsten beads.

I like a leader with an average length of 18 to 20 feet, with a 3- or 4-weight rod that's 10 or 11 feet long. I typically fish my two flies anywhere from 24 to 30 inches apart, tying the dropper on a 4- to 6-inch dropper tag and placing my Woven Mayfly in either the point or dropper tag position based upon where the fish are feeding in the water column. A typical tuck cast upstream will jettison my flies so that they enter the water on a tight line. I'll immediately begin my drift as they enter the water. When fishing directly upstream, the drifts are typically short, but when I fish at a 45-degree angle up and across, I can fish a much larger expanse of water, often to a position downstream from where I'm standing. On some days when the fish are up in the heads of the runs, I'll consistently catch fish within the first few feet of my drift. This is usually true during periods of high insect activity, as trout will often move into the most opportune feeding lie. At other times when the insect activity is dwindling, the fish may be in the transitional areas of a particular run, and I'll often have to fish a longer drift to catch them.

The Woven Mayfly has produced in a plethora of water conditions throughout the year. Although I designed the fly for periods of hatching activity, it has proven to be a solid searching pattern during periods of little to no activity. This fly is not just a Northeastern pattern; I have had many customers use these on Western streams with resounding success fished in all of the methods listed above, taking a variety of species of trout.

The Woven Mayfly Nymph can be a sound substitute for any size of stonefly nymph. Often, I carry larger versions using a pair of tungsten beads like this size 6. Stonefly nymphs often reside in heavier more turbulent water requiring the added weight.

Variations

I rarely leave home during trout season without a variety of these flies in different colors and sizes, as I often encounter hatches of medium to large mayflies and stoneflies on the streams I frequent. If I need a really heavy fly, then I will double up a pair of the larger sized beads to ensure that the fly will get down. When the water is off color and high, I find the bigger the fly, the better, and that a darker or brighter color will work, too. If I know I'll face these conditions, I will often tie a few with pronounced hot spot collars of Datum Glo Brite in shades of chartreuse, red, or bright orange as they have a tendency to work well and act as a trigger.

DARK BROWN WOVEN MAYFLY NYMPH

Hook:	#6-14 Gamakatsu S10-B, Tiemco 5262
Bead:	Copper tungsten, size to match
Thread:	Cream 140-denier Ultra Thread
Underbody:	6 to 10 turns round lead wire
Tail:	Medium pardo Coq de Leon
Abdomen:	Dark brown #3031 over pale yellow #707 DMC Embroidery Yarn
Rib:	Amber Ultra Wire (Brassie)
Wing Case:	Brown Hareline Flashyback
Legs:	March Brown Brahma hen
Thorax:	Cream Hareline Dubbin

Note: Use .010" lead wire for the underbody for #12-14 and .015" for #6-10. Tie the abdomen with a shuttle weave.

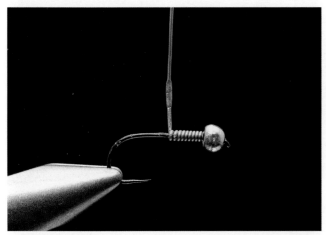

1. Bead the hook, affix the hook in the vise, and add a small drop of superglue to the hook shank directly behind the bead. Attach the round lead wire behind the bead, and work eight to ten turns down the hook shank. When you reach the midway point of the hook, flatten out the wire with a pair of non-serrated wires, building a taper as shown in the picture.

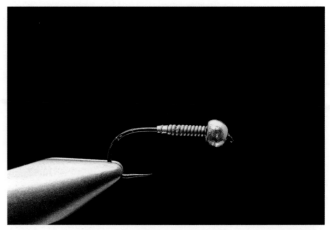

2. Wrap the tapered end of the lead wire on the shank, and break off the wire at the end of the flattened section. This little trick helps build in a nice taper to the fly without having to use an excessive amount of thread.

3. Attach the tying thread behind the bead, and work your way toward the rear of the underbody, making sure to cover up as much of the lead wire as possible.

4. Remove a small section of six to eight barbs off of a Coq de Leon feather and secure them to the top of the hook. Continue your thread wraps to the point where the hook bend starts. Lift the tail fibers up, and take one turn of thread behind and underneath the tail to prop the fibers up.

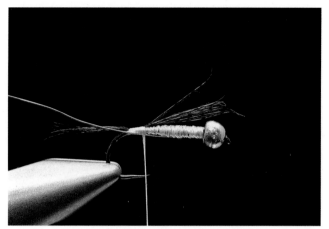

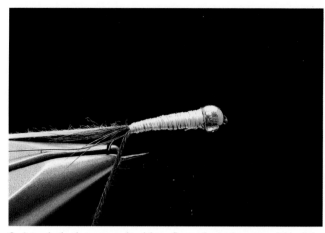

5. Affix the wire ribbing material to the near side of the hook with a couple of loose thread wraps. After making a couple of turns of thread, maneuver the wire rib to the center of the underside of the fly.

8. Attach the brown embroidery floss along the near side of the hook and wrap the thread rearward toward the tail of the fly. After securing the floss to the near side of the hook, return your tying thread to a position behind the bead, whip-finish, and clip the thread.

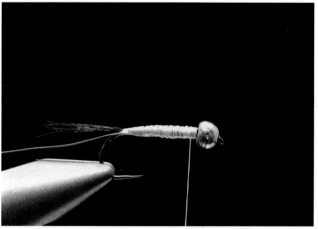

6. Continue covering the wire rib and butt ends of the Coq de Leon with your tying thread until the thread is behind the bead.

9. Turn the vise so that you are facing the front of the fly, and grab each of the bobbins spooled with the embroidery floss. This is a two-handed exercise and requires you to maintain equal tension on the floss throughout. The brown (top color) should be in your left hand, and the pale yellow (bottom) should be in your right hand. Take your left hand and pass the floss over the top of the rear of the fly.

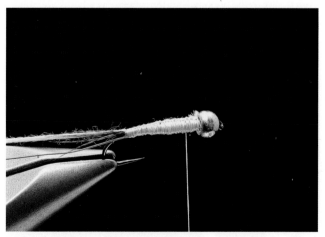

7. Attach the pale yellow embroidery floss along the far side of the hook and wrap the thread rearward toward the tail of the fly. After securing the floss to the far side of the hook, return your tying thread to a position behind the bead.

10. While keeping the floss short from the bobbin and maintaining pressure, take the pale yellow bobbin and go over the top of the brown floss, down the front, and under the bottom of the body of the fly. The key to keeping the weave together is keeping the pressure on the floss on either side of the fly while keeping the amount of floss from the bobbin to the fly body short.

11. While maintaining pressure on both bobbins, bring the brown floss back over the top of the fly in the other direction, maintaining the same level of tension on the floss. If you let go of the floss, or decrease the tension on either piece, the weave will shift.

12. Bring the yellow floss over the top of the brown floss from the tail and then down in front of the brown floss and directly under the fly to the other side. Now you have completed a series of weaves on either side of the fly.

13. Continue the same sequences in the last four steps, repeatedly working your way toward the front of the fly. This picture is a good depiction of how long the section of floss should be from the fly to the bobbin. Shorter is better as it helps you maintain solid tension throughout the weaving process.

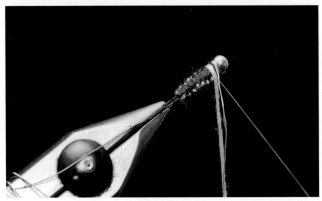

14. When you reach a position roughly an eye's length behind the bead, cross both sections of floss over the top of the fly, and let the bobbins hang. This will keep tension on the floss as you reattach the tying thread behind the bead.

One of the inspirations for the Synthetic Quill Nymph came from Kevin Compton's Tungsten Torpedo, which is a slender, thread-bodied nymph with a double rib of holographic tinsel and wire creating a distinctly segmented body. The Torpedo is tied with a wing case so it has a distinct top and bottom to the pattern. A simple change in material colors, and you can cover pretty much any medium to smaller mayfly nymph you encounter.

I really liked Kevin's pattern and thought I could make it a quick tie so that I could easily replenish my stocks for guiding. I quickly learned that the average tailwater trout's diet consisted of smaller nymphs on a regular basis, and in order to catch these trout, I needed to become adept at fishing smaller subsurface imitations.

Because my home waters receive tremendous amounts of fishing pressure every season, I found that fishing flies that were subtly different from what everyone else was fishing often provided success. My thoughts after seeing the Tungsten Torpedo were to make a pattern that had a similar segmented body but was tied in the round without a definitive top or bottom. At the time I had been doing well with longer French-style nymph systems and was looking for a quick micro nymph that I wouldn't feel so bad losing, as a typical guide day might see a half dozen or more flies disappear on snags or broken-off fish.

In my product orders from Kevin, he would always generously toss in a couple of extra products that might be new to his store or something that he thought I might have some use for. In an order of literally thousands of tungsten beads, Kevin put in a package of Synthetic Quill Body by Fly DK, a European company of fly-tying materials. I took one look at this material and wasn't impressed. I remember pitching the package to a corner of my tying desk, where it sat for a few days. After a week went by, I got an email from Kevin out of the blue, and he asked about my thoughts on the material. I was honest with Kevin, and told him I hadn't used it yet and wasn't sure if I would have any need for it. Kevin hinted subtly that it wasn't just a flashy material and that I should open it up and take a look at it. Figuring that Kevin must clearly know something that I didn't, I grabbed the package that evening and had a look for myself.

Once I opened up the cellophane and pulled out a section, I realized I was wrong in my initial assessment of the material. Synthetic Quill Body is similar to a stripped peacock quill in that it has a natural ridge on one side. Once it's tied in on a hook, you can actually build a segmented effect similar to that of a stripped quill, with the only difference being it has a bit more of flash built into the material. The Synthetic Quill Body was a godsend: you could put a tremendous amount of pressure on it while wrapping it up the hook without having to worry about it breaking. At the time, we were in the thick of the trout season, and a plethora of smaller insects were hatching daily. We'd see anything, including Sulphurs, Olives, Chocolate Duns, Micro Stones, and even Tricos, on a daily basis. Most of the naturals ranged in colors from olive to brown to almost black.

The water conditions that particular summer were good, our reservoirs were full, and the MDC was running steady flows of 350 to 425 cfs from the Hogback Dam. Those flows

Synthetic Quill Body is a UV-hued material that can change color depending on the color of thread in the underbody.

put just enough water in the river to spread the fish out while also giving the angler comfortable wading. For weeks, I had been catching the bulk of my fish in the heads of the riffles and pockets with weighted nymphs fished on a tight line. My rig of choice was a 16-foot leader to a modified French coiled sighter, and anywhere from 4 to 8 feet of straight 5X fluorocarbon tippet to my flies, which were then 30 inches apart on the same sized fluorocarbon tippet. When I say modified coil, I mean a lightly coiled sighter, one that is approximately 8 to 12 inches long with approximately 4 to 6 open coils across the length of the sighter. Overall, I prefer my coiled sighters this way, as I feel they are a much more versatile and will allow me to transition to a variety of Euro nymphing fishing styles. I like versatility whenever fishing; if I have to waste valuable time changing out an entire leader system to fish different styles of flies, it takes away from time spent catching fish. That morning I began fishing with my new patterns as droppers off of 4- to 6-inch dropper tags with a heavier fly as an anchor. Because there was limited surface activity to start the day, I began fishing in the buckets of the runs, as I figured the fish might not be up in the shallow riffles and heads of the pools until the insect activity increased.

As luck would have it, several Chocolate Duns and Olives were beginning to emerge, so I began working my way to the head of a promising riffle and started to consistently pick off trout on the little nymph I had tied the night prior. As the day wore on, and the insect activity remained consistent, I continued to catch several trout of all sizes on this simple pattern. Once the sun got a bit higher, I found that the fly with the hot spot collar became much more effective than the one tied without. By mid afternoon I had tallied several dozen fish, with the smallest trout measuring 8 inches all the way up to a robust 19-inch, hook-jawed, male brown trout.

That summer I tied the fly in shades of olive, brown, and dark brown, or a combination of these, and fished them all over the Northeast. I remember one day when my friend Mike and I were fishing the Upper West Branch of the Delaware River during Sulphur time where we literally caught somewhere around sixty to seventy fish that day. We were frantically switching back and forth between a black pattern and a brown pattern all day. Once one fly stopped working, we'd change colors, and the action would continue again. That was one of the most memorable days I've ever experienced on that particular fishery, and one that I have yet to match to this day.

As the season progressed, the Synthetic Quill Nymph earned its keep in my rotation of nymph patterns. I found myself fishing this pattern with clients and on my own personal excursions regularly, and throughout the entire season. Anytime I found moderate flows, fairly clear water, and smaller bugs, the fly would consistently catch fish. It has done well on a variety of fisheries in the Northeast as well as a variety of other locales across the country. Pretty much anywhere you encounter smaller bugs, the Synthetic Quill Nymph will habitually catch fish.

Fishing

I have caught fish on the Synthetic Quill Nymph using a variety of techniques, but my initial intent was to build a smaller weighted micro nymph to be fished in a tight-line or indicator nymph-fishing system. My first experiences with this pattern were solely in a longer leader French system using a coiled sighter indicator. As I stated earlier, this particular system thrives in shallow riffles and pockets and is based on the premise of fishing lightly weighted flies from a distance and almost entirely at an immediate upstream angle. The drifts are short, sometimes as little as a foot, to as long as 10 feet, depending on the length of your leader, and most competitive anglers who employ this technique will often tell you that they work a drift to a three count, set the hook, and cast their flies again. It's a systematic approach to nymph fishing, breaking the stretch of water you are on into a grid, trying to put your flies in every possible area upstream of your position. The key to the technique is stopping your rod tip high on the forward cast so that the flies enter the water first, and begin tracking your flies back toward your position as they enter the water. If you're in contact

Angler Tommy Baranowski takes a low position while nymphing a nice run under low, clear conditions during the summer. Smaller weighted nymphs under these conditions can be the ticket to success.

with your flies as soon as they enter the water and throughout the course of your working drift, you'll detect the takes easily as the coiled sighter will either straighten out and stop, or you will get such a violent take that that you'll feel it in the rod tip. How far you intend to stay away from the water you're targeting will dictate the overall length of your leader.

The trick is to simply fish at a distance that will still allow you the room to manipulate your flies correctly while not spooking the fish in the run. When insect activity is dense, and the fish are actively feeding in the riffles, the takes are almost instantaneous. Many times as the fly is descending in the water column upon the initial cast, it will get eaten by the fish. This at first seems a little out of the ordinary, as you'd think that nymphs being bottom-dwelling organisms will naturally ascend the water column, and thus be readily eaten in that manner. But trust me when I say that, under those circumstances when trout are actively feeding in a shallow riffle, you'll be amazed at how many fish you'll catch as your flies enter the water.

These methods thrive during periods of high insect activity when trout are eating heavily on smaller nymphs in the heads of major pools, riffles, and pocketwater. These situations are often met during periods when the waters are in the ideal temperatures for trout, which is usually from April through November in the Northeast. You have a little more leeway when fishing on spring creeks and tailwater fisheries, where the temperature swings are much less drastic and you may never encounter water that dips below 40 degrees. This seems to be a general baseline from my experiences, but many other variables can affect your success. Some hatches where I have found this pattern to work well are Sulphurs, Pale Morning or Evening Duns, Chocolate Duns, Blue-Winged Olives, Tricos, Little Winter Stones, Yellow Sallies, and various types of midges. If you are in the midst of any of these hatches, the Synthetic Quill Nymph can be a very effective fly.

Although French nymphing is a deadly technique under the right conditions, you can be successful fishing the Synthetic Quill Nymph under an indicator or as a dropper under a highly buoyant dry fly. Since the pattern is tied in the round, it makes a good attractor or general pattern, which in my estimate could easily be taken for a variety of different insects including mayflies, midges, or stoneflies. Whenever I tied up a few of these flies for myself or for clients, I always made sure to have some with and without hot spot collars, and also some that were tied with tungsten and brass beads for the various water types I might encounter.

Like any of the nymph patterns I fish with, I really don't think that there is a right or wrong technique to fish them. A few minor alterations in weight or material, and you can fish this fly in a variety of disciplines. The trick is to assess the water that you are about to fish and determine what technique you think will be most effective based upon where the fish are feeding in the water column.

Variations

There are several different colors of the Synthetic Quill Body, but actually the UV Pearl color is the only color you really need. A change in thread color will alter the appearance of the material, or add just enough flash to the pattern overall. The graphite color is my favorite, as it blends well with multiple colors as well, most notably the darker hues such as black, gray, or olive. Earth tones that I mentioned earlier are by far my favorite and most successful color combinations, but at other times and conditions gaudy color combinations will be effective. I've had competitive anglers request color combinations in shades of red, purple, and chartreuse as attractor patterns for use in a variety of water conditions. In addition to the Partridge Sproat Wet hook model in the recipe, I sometimes will tie it on a curved scud or grub hook to achieve a slightly different appearance

BLACK SYNTHETIC QUILL NYMPH

Hook:	#14-16 Partridge Sproat Wet
Bead:	Black tungsten, size to match
Thread:	Black 70- or 140-denier Ultra Thread
Tail:	Coq de Leon
Rib 1:	Silver Ultra Wire (small or x-small)
Rib 2:	Synthetic Quill Body
Thorax:	Black mole fur or Hareline Microfine Dubbing

Note: You can substitute a #14-20 Tiemco 100 for the hook.

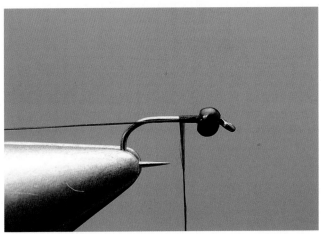

1. Bead the hook and place it in the vise. Begin wrapping the tying thread directly behind the bead, and continue wrapping to the midway point of the hook.

2. Strip four to six fibers from a Coq de Leon feather, keeping the tips aligned. Measure the fibers to the length of the hook shank, and tie them in on top of the hook. Work the thread toward the rear of the fly. When you reach the bend of the hook, lift up the tails and make one thread wrap under the tail to prop up the fibers.

3. Measure the silver wire rib, place it at a 45-degree angle to the fly, and begin wrapping your thread over the wire only taking one turn of thread.

4. Lay a section of Synthetic Quill Body on top of the wire, and secure the material with a quick turn or two of thread.

5. Continue wrapping the thread forward toward the bead. After taking four or five turns of thread over the materials, trim the butt ends of the tail, as well as the two ribbing materials just behind the bead. Wrap the thread forward to the bead making sure to cover the materials evenly.

6. Begin wrapping the Synthetic Quill Body forward toward the bead of the hook in even and open wraps. The key is to allow enough space between the wraps to expose the thread underbody as well as leave room for the wire ribbing.

7. Start wrapping the wire for the second rib. Start your first turn under the tail at the rear of the fly before wrapping through the fly pattern.

8. Wrap the wire rib forward in between the wraps of synthetic quill body to make a multi-colored abdomen. Once you reach the bead, secure the ribbing with four to six turns of thread to build a base for the next step.

9. Dub a thin noodle of mole or Microfine Dubbing to the thread. Due to the fly's small size, the dubbing noodle should be no longer than an inch.

10. Wrap the dubbing noodle directly behind the bead. It should take only two or three full turns to make your collar. Anything more than that will overdress the fly.

11. After completing your collar, whip-finish the thread and cement the thread wraps with your cement of choice. Standing alone, this is a durable micro nymph, but if you wish, you can also cover the body with cement or UV resin prior to tying in the collar, but this is completely optional.

DARK OLIVE SYNTHETIC QUILL NYMPH

Hook: #14-16 Partridge Sproat Wet
Bead: Nickel tungsten, size to match
Thread: Olive brown 70- or 140-denier Ultra Thread
Tail: Coq de Leon
Rib 1:   Green Ultra Wire (small or x-small)
Rib 2:   Synthetic Quill Body
Thorax: Dark olive Hareline Dubbin

Note: You can substitute a #14-20 Tiemco 100 for the hook.

LIGHT OLIVE SYNTHETIC QUILL NYMPH

Hook: #14-16 Partridge Sproat Wet
Bead: Gold tungsten, size to match
Thread: Olive 70- or 140-denier Ultra Thread
Tail: Coq de Leon
Rib #1:   Gold Ultra Wire (small or x-small)
Rib #2:   Synthetic Quill Body
Thorax: Light olive Hareline Dubbin

Note: You can substitute a #14-20 Tiemco 100 for the hook.

GRAY SYNTHETIC QUILL NYMPH

Hook: #14-16 Partridge Sproat Wet
Bead: Silver tungsten, size to match
Thread: Gray-brown 70- or 140-denier Ultra Thread
Tail: Coq de Leon
Rib 1:   Black Ultra Wire (small or x-small)
Rib 2:   Synthetic Quill Body
Thorax: Light gray Hareline Dubbin

Note: You can substitute a #14-20 Tiemco 100 for the hook.

BROWN SYNTHETIC QUILL NYMPH

Hook: #14-16 Partridge Sproat Wet
Bead: Copper tungsten, size to match
Thread: Rusty brown 70- or 140-denier Ultra Thread
Tail: Coq de Leon
Rib 1:   Copper brown Ultra Wire (small or x-small)
Rib 2:   Synthetic Quill Body

Note: You can substitute a #14-20 Tiemco 100 for the hook.

CHAPTER 15

Quill Bodied Jig

Jig nymphs became popular in competition circles, originally in the Czech Republic, and have only become popular in the United States in the last decade or so. The interesting thing about jigs in Europe is they are considered to be more a style of nymph than anything else. If you research many of the patterns that originate from Europe, they have generic names built primarily around the materials that they are made from. Often, they are named after the colors that they have in them, like the Tanned Pink Tail Goldhead. It is nothing more than a pink-tailed jig with synthetic peacock dubbing, tan colored hen hackle, and a gold bead. Most of the patterns that are tied and fished on jig

By simply changing the color of the bead, thread, wire, or dubbing, you can create a plethora of color combinations off of the same Quill Bodied Jig pattern recipe.

hooks are tied in the round. Few patterns incorporate a distinct wing case or shellback.

Jig-hook-tied flies are some of the most interesting and effective fly patterns that I have had the opportunity to fish with, and they open another style of fly pattern to experiment with.

Jigs tied with even the tiniest amount of weight will track with the hook point up as long as the weight is positioned in the front of the hook. This makes for flies that are less apt to hang up or snag the bottom. Grub or scud hooks, if weighted properly, will do the same thing, inverting in the water column, riding with the hook point up. Although many popular nymph patterns have been converted to some jig hooks, I have found that suggestive attractors tied in the round have worked consistently.

Jigs are a perfect candidate for longer leader French or Spanish tight-line set up, since they don't require an exorbitant amount of weight to get into a trout's feeding zone, especially in shallow, clear water. Often a small tungsten bead of $^1/8$-inch diameter or smaller will do the trick with no extra lead wire

affixed to the shank of the hook. They will also accommodate beads one or two sizes larger than what is typically used on them so going heavier is made easy when necessary.

The Quill Bodied Jig is yet another elementary fly pattern that came together quickly. My thoughts were simple: barred tail, tapered ribbed or textured abdomen, with a collar/thorax of muted flash with some sort of buggy dubbing or webby hen feather for legs, followed by a tungsten bead for a head. By making the abdomen tapered and using something soft for a buggy thorax, the idea was to make a fly that would plummet through the water column quickly to get into a trout's feeding zone. I'm sure the basic design has been tied and thought up by many, but it's worth demonstrating my take on it.

I was never a fan of using natural stripped quills for bodies, as they were often brittle and would break when wrapping them on the hook shank. Stripped Peacock Eye Quills by Polish Quills are some of the finest dyed quills I've worked with. They're pliable, come in a slew of colors, and make fantastic segmented bodies on nymphs, dry flies, and wets. If you have

Jig patterns are proven fish-catchers and often a great option for an anchor in a tight-line nymph rig, as they typically ride with the hook point facing upward reducing the number of snags. This brown trout fell for an olive Quill Bodied Jig during a heavy hatch of Blue-Winged Olives.

You can develop a wide spectrum of variations off of a single jig hook. Here are five versions of the same size 12 Quill Bodied Jig. The three on the left are all with varying sized tungsten beads with the top being the heaviest with a $5/32$-inch faceted bead, the middle with a $1/8$-inch unfaceted bead, and bottom with a $7/64$-inch unfaceted bead. The jigs on the right use the same sized bead but show two popular positions for the hot spot.

problems with the quills being too brittle and breaking, a trick to make them more pliable is to work a little vegetable oil into the quills before tying, and they will regain their pliability.

Stripped Peacock Quills provide segmentation to a fly because they have two-toned coloring. One edge of the quill is usually much darker than the other, and when wrapped on the shank of a hook, gives a realistic, bug-like appearance to your fly. The key to making a uniformly tapered cone shaped abdomen relies heavily on tapering your lead underbody. A little trick that has helped in reassuring this on every one that I tie is simply tapering the end of the lead wire with a pair of flat pliers. Because of their natural barring, and their stiff and thin diameter, I stuck with Coq de Leon for the tailing material on this pattern.

To add a little bit of spice to this pattern, I decided on building an in the round abdomen using two different types of dubbing. To represent legs, I figured I'd add a buggy dubbing with a fair amount of guard hairs in the mix. Any type of squirrel blend or hare's ear blend will suffice for the collar, but I wasn't satisfied with using just one dubbing for this section of the fly. I tinkered around with a couple of different blends until I found what I was looking for. I eventually settled on a pinch of Ice Dub behind a collar of any sort of buggy dubbing. The flash from the Ice Dub would be subdued by the larger coarser dubbing, and I later found it worked well.

Fishing

Whether used with a short- or long-line European technique, these particular styles of nymphs excel, in that they get down in the water column and have an enticing action to trout as they jig and bounce through the water column on a drift. Where you choose to put your jig in your team of flies will depend on how the fish are feeding. Once I have the color and size that the fish are eating, I may fish two of the same fly for the rest of the day until their effectiveness diminishes. Sometimes, using the same-colored jig in two different sizes is a great searching tactic, especially if you're anticipating a specific hatch of insects to occur.

In the winter, jigs are deadly for sluggish and wary trout, and you can employ them in an indicator system with great effectiveness, or actively along the bottom. When using a tungsten-weighted jig in a two-fly indicator system, you can have a precise suspension system that typically won't require the use of any extra split shot in the system. Because many times in the winter fish will take up residence in slower seams, soft edges, and often water with some depth, the weight of the jig will be all that you need to get your flies into the zone where the trout are holding. The key to fishing these types of water is to stack mend your line as your flies progress downstream of your position to ensure a drag-free drift. Lightly weighted jigs can be effective under a greased-coiled sighter as well, and often when I need a stealthy nymph system, this is my preferred method. Often in the winter when fish are keying in on some of the smaller Winter Stonefly nymphs, I will pair a Quill Bodied Jig with an Infant Stone and pick up fish throughout the day.

To more actively fish your jig, remove any indicators and droppers, and fish a single jig crawled slowly along the bottom. Cast your fly into a shallow run, and allow it time to sink to the bottom. Once your fly is on the bottom, begin your retrieve with a slight strip of the line or continually move the fly back to your position with a hand twist. This can be an effective method in some of the slower regions of a stream or in a stillwater setting.

Variations

As with all jig patterns, I prefer to weight the Quill Bodied Jig with slotted tungsten beads so that the bead can pass the elbow of the jig hook and seat firmly to the hook eye. As I mentioned, you can also go much larger or smaller than normal with slotted beads, as they clear the bend much easier than standard beads.

Color combinations are up to you, but I've listed some of my favorites at the end of the chapter. Hot spots on these flies are easy to incorporate, as the patterns are tied in the round. You can make the hot spots small by adding a few turns of Datum Glo Brite in the tail of the fly or at the collar behind the bead. It takes only a couple extra seconds to add a hot spot while tying them, and it will give you a little more variety in your box to choose from.

Another viable alternative in design for this pattern is using hen feathers or CDC for legs. CDC, my first choice, has excellent movement and is mostly associated with wings for dry flies. Because of its light, airy appearance, CDC is an excellent choice for legs on nymphs, especially jigs. The only alteration you need to make to the pattern is to simply add a couple of turns of CDC in the collar. The most durable way to do this is to strip the fibers from the stems of the CDC feathers and either place them in a dubbing loop or split the tying thread and spin them into a rope. Once your loop is complete, simply wrap the CDC collar and preen the fibers toward the back of the fly, whip-finish, and you're done. CDC has great natural movement in the water, and can be the difference in enticing a trout to strike, as it gives off the appearance of a living organism.

If you're looking for a leg material with a more natural barring that isn't as soft as CDC, then I recommend a couple turns of Brahma hen or partridge. These two feathers offer up an entirely different effect to the fly and make the jig reminiscent of a weighted soft hackle. These flies are just a template. Use the materials that you prefer, experiment, and have fun.

RUSTY BROWN QUILL BODIED JIG	
Hook:	#8-18 Partridge Patriot Ideal Jig
Bead:	Copper slotted tungsten, size to match
Thread:	Rusty brown 70- or 140-denier Ultra Thread
Tail:	Coq de Leon
Body:	Brown Polish Quill
Rib:	Amber Ultra Wire (small)
Abdomen:	Rusty brown Ice Dub, and brown Spiky Squirrel or Hareline Dubbin

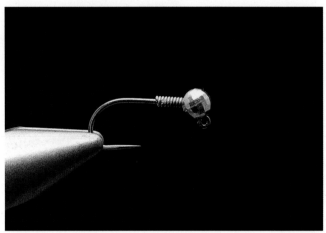

1. Slide a slotted tungsten bead onto the hook, seating the bead against the eye. Take a section of round lead wire, and then make six to eight turns on the hook shank, clip the ends, and push the section up into the slot of the bead to ensure it doesn't move. A small drop of superglue over the wraps of lead will also help prevent it from rolling.

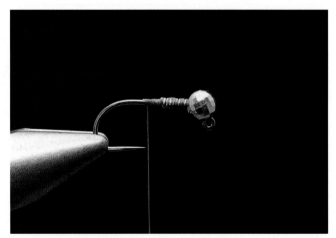

2. Attach the tying thread directly behind the section of lead wire, and make several wraps, forming a cone-shaped ramp to the lead. Take a few turns forward over the wraps of lead, and then return the thread to a place in line with the point of the hook.

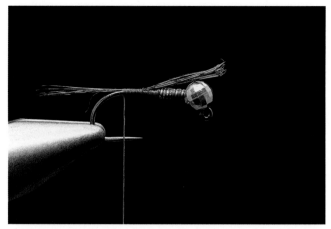

3. Peel six to eight fibers from a Coq de Leon feather, measure them to the hook shank, and tie them in on the top of the hook, advancing the thread to the start of the bend.

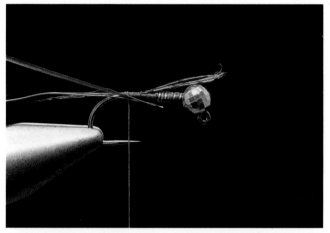

4. To speed up the tying process, take the wire rib and the Polish Quill, and tie them in simultaneously. The quill should be on top of the wire since you will wrap it on the shank first.

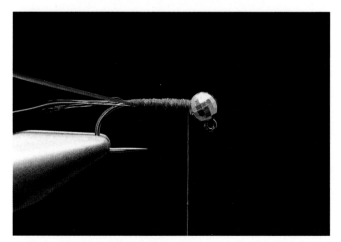

5. Cover the lead wire underbody entirely with tying thread while building a neat, evenly cone-shaped underbody. This will make wrapping the quill much easier on the next step.

6. Begin wrapping the quill forward in even, open wraps, leaving the thread exposed in between each wrap. Wrap the quill to a point right behind the bead, and tie it off with a half hitch. If you neglect the half hitch, the quill runs the risk of unraveling.

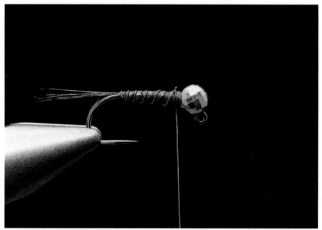

7. Begin wrapping the wire rib forward in between the sections of the quill. If done correctly, you should have a multi-colored and multi-textured effect from the thread, quill, and wire. Like the previous step with the quills, secure the wire and half hitch the thread to prevent it from unraveling.

8. To make a more durable fly, coat the body with a layer of head cement or Clear Cure Goo Hydro, and cure it with a UV torch.

9. Dub a small noodle of Ice Dub on the thread and wrap a small bulb behind the bead. The small bundle of Ice Dub will add a little flash to the fly while also helping to prop up the next section of dubbing.

10. Like the Rock Candy Larva, split the thread and add some Hareline Dubbin or Spiky Squirrel dubbing between the sections of thread.

11. Spin the thread to create a dubbing loop and wrap the dubbing directly behind the bead. You should use a short section of dubbing that uses two to three turns of material. This section of dubbing should represent the legs, and if done correctly, will bleed into the rear of the fly.

12. Finish the fly with a four-turn whip-finish and cement the thread wraps. If there are any errant fibers from the collar, tease or pick them out with a piece of velcro.

DARK BROWN QUILL BODIED JIG

Hook:	#8-18 Partridge Patriot Ideal Jig
Bead:	Copper slotted tungsten, size to match
Thread:	Dark brown 70- or 140-denier Ultra Thread
Tail:	Coq de Leon
Body:	Brown Polish Quill
Rib:	Amber Ultra Wire (small)
Abdomen:	Pheasant tail Ice Dub, and brown Spiky Squirrel or Hareline Dubbin

LIGHT OLIVE QUILL BODIED JIG

Hook:	#8-18 Partridge Patriot Ideal Jig
Bead:	Gold slotted tungsten, size to match
Thread:	Light olive 6/0 or 8/0 Uni-Thread
Tail:	Coq de Leon
Body:	Light olive Polish Quill
Rib:	Black Ultra Wire (small)
Abdomen:	Olive Ice Dub, and light olive Spiky Squirrel or Hareline Dubbin

YELLOW QUILL BODIED JIG

Hook:	#8-18 Partridge Patriot Ideal Jig
Bead:	Gold slotted tungsten, size to match
Thread:	Yellow 70- or 140-denier Ultra Thread
Tail:	Coq de Leon
Body:	Yellow Polish Quill
Rib:	Black Ultra Wire (small)
Abdomen:	Hot yellow Ice Dub, and golden Spiky Squirrel or Hareline Hare-Tron Dubbin

DARK OLIVE QUILL BODIED JIG

Hook:	#8-18 Partridge Patriot Ideal Jig
Bead:	Nickel slotted tungsten, size to match
Thread:	Olive-brown 70- or 140-denier Ultra Thread
Tail:	Coq de Leon
Body:	Olive Polish Quill
Rib:	Silver Ultra Wire (small)
Abdomen:	Olive Ice Dub, and dark olive Spiky Squirrel or Hareline Dubbin

HARE'S EAR QUILL BODIED JIG

Hook:	#8-18 Partridge Patriot Ideal Jig
Bead:	Metallic red slotted tungsten, size to match
Thread:	Gray-brown 70- or 140-denier Ultra Thread
Tail:	Coq de Leon
Body:	Natural Polish Quill
Rib:	Red Ultra Wire (small)
Abdomen:	Pheasant tail Ice Dub, and natural Spiky Squirrel or Hareline Dubbin

CHAPTER 16

Shimmer Stone

If I could fish only one nymph all the time, I would always pick a stonefly. Since stoneflies are typically some of, if not the largest subsurface insect in any given stream, it's safe to say that they're a tough meal to pass up for even the wisest of fish. Early on, I learned how important the stonefly nymph is in any serious trout fisherman's arsenal, and it has become a staple in all of my nymph boxes.

Many rivers have healthy populations of a variety of species and sizes of stoneflies. Even when stoneflies are not present in a particular watershed, fishing a medium to large stonefly

Larger stonefly nymphs have a distinctive shape that is often problematic to replicate on a hook. Once you find a good pattern, as I did with the Shimmer Stone, keep a variety of colors in your selection.

nymph will fool a fish or two even under the toughest of conditions. I recall several outings where the going was tough and a stonefly imitation saved the day when nothing else would.

Most larger stones have life cycles that span up to four years. Having such a long lifespan makes them a readily available food source pretty much any day of the year. Many of the larger stoneflies crawl out of the water to hatch, and some will hatch in the cover of darkness. The nymphs typically inhabit fast water with high levels of oxygenation and generally don't drift freely in the current unless they become dislodged from their surroundings from a change in flow.

Aside from periods of activity or metamorphosis, there are a few other times when my first choice is to tie on a stonefly. When faced with above average flows, rising or receding waters, lower visibility in the water column, or a combination of all three, I will tie a stonefly on as a lead fly, or sometimes I'll even tie on a pair of stones. I like to have a variety of flies at my disposal, as these complex insects will vary in size and color as a result of where they are in their life cycle and what surroundings they inhabit.

On many of the waters in my area, stonefly nymph patterns are a staple throughout the winter as well. With fewer insects available than at other times of the year, the fish will become more opportunistic feeders. When the water level fluctuates, stonefly nymphs are some of the biggest meals that are let loose in the drift, and trout have a difficult time passing them up. I developed my Shimmer Stone nymph one winter in hopes of creating a go-to stonefly nymph that could be fished in a variety of ways and situations.

Because stonefly nymphs are large, complex insects, they provide several challenges for the fly tier. To represent them correctly with an effective pattern, you need to look at the insect closely. If you look at large stonefly species, you'll see they have some distinct characteristics, which I feel need to be included in the construction of an imitation. Consumers can choose from several really good patterns that have distinct segmented abdomens and pronounced thoracic plates and legs. The balance of the patterns seem to fall into one of two categories: suggestive and realistic.

The suggestive patterns are typically tied in the round and have a large profile. In my experience, these types of patterns fish well in fast, broken water, but their effectiveness tapers off when fished in slower environs. The realistic patterns that are available seem to fish well in both environs, but they are more time-consuming to construct. When I decided to tackle the project of designing a new stonefly nymph imitation, I wanted something realistic enough to resemble the natural, but with some suggestive triggers built into the design to give it extra fish-catching attributes. I also wanted to add some materials in this fly's construction that would give the impression of life.

The next obstacle to overcome was creating a fly with a natural profile. A stonefly tapers from head to tail, while also maintaining a flat profile, most likely to aid in keeping the bug affixed to the bottom or allowing it to crawl around between rocks on the stream bed. This insect has distinct sections: the thorax has three distinct thoracic plates, three oversized pairs of legs, and an abdomen with heavy segmentation. They also

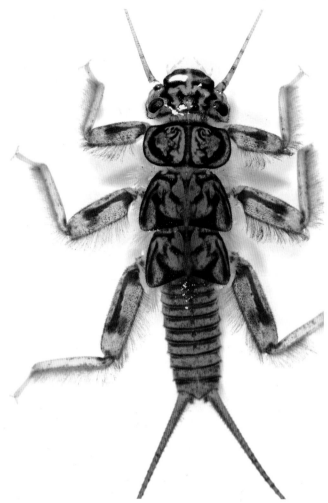

Golden Stonefly nymphs are some of the largest nymphs in any stream, and so they are regularly eaten by trout whenever they are available. JOHN MILLER

have a distinctly dark or mottled back with a lighter colored underbelly, which is visible as they tumble along in the drift.

A fly that always intrigued me growing up was George Grant's Woven Stonefly. The pattern is tied in the round, but the woven body emphasizes the distinct two-toned color change of the naturals and is, in my opinion, the trigger in this time-tested pattern. I, too, in the beginning phases of my pattern's construction, felt that this was something that needed to be included in the design of a fly.

Seeing as how stonefly nymphs come from the streambed in fast water, it was imperative that I incorporate some weight into my fly's design, but not so much weight that it would habitually hang bottom. I decided to incorporate a copper bead and a lead-free wire in the fly's underbody. Round lead-free wire, after being affixed to the hook, can easily be shaped after being covered with a layer of thread. I decided to cover the lead-free wire with Uni-Stretch rather than using thread, as it would be quicker and use less material.

The antennae and tails on the fly needed to be streamlined, as they are longer and thinner than the legs and are important in the fly's construction. I decided to use a synthetic material to

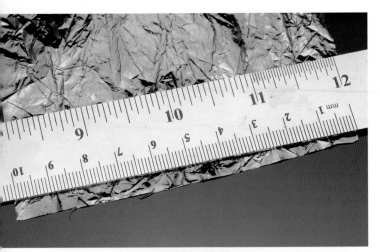

Hareline Flashyback is a reflective cellophane-type material that cuts easily with a ruler and razor. For the Shimmer Stone, cut your strips ahead of time with a slight taper from one end.

Hareline's D-Rib has extreme elasticity, easily stretching to twice its static length without breaking.

Brahma hen capes are excellent for tailing and leg fibers for nymph patterns. The fibers have natural barring and are much more durable than partridge feathers. A cape like this retails for $20 and can tie hundreds of flies.

represent these appendages, and I opted for Life Flex by Hareline. (Flexi Floss and Spanflex are two of the several alternatives on the market that readily come to mind.) I chose Life Flex, as it seemed to have the color ranges that I was looking for, and it was readily available.

To make the fly with a distinctly darker top and lighter bottom, I had a slew of options. I wanted a product that would reflect light, since I'd had success from time to time with nymphs that had some sort of flash built into their wing cases. Additionally, I felt that the flash had to run across the entire top portion of the fly, and it had to be durable. Durability is a huge factor for me, especially when I am designing a fly that is going to be rolled along the bottom. I settled on Hareline's Flashyback because it is a cellophane material that comes in a sheet and is easy to cut with an exacto knife and a ruler into the desired shape.

Segmentation in the abdomen was another important attribute for my pattern design. D-Rib completed the segmented effect nicely, and made the rear section of the fly virtually indestructible. D-Rib is a half round stretchy material that is rather easy to work with, translucent and highly durable. To this day, I have yet to have this section of the fly come apart, even after several hours of fishing and countless numbers of trout.

To fortify the exposed Flashyback material on the thoracic region, I coat the sections with a thin layer of Clear Cure Goo Hydro. I used Hare-Tron Dubbin for the underbelly in the thoracic regions, as I am a huge proponent of any dubbing with a little Antron and rabbit fur. The two combined provide both light reflection and movement, giving the appearance of life. The legs were the last ingredient in the pattern, and they are represented with three sections of Brahma hen, tapered to accurately represent the legs of the natural.

Fishing

If I had only one size to choose from in my fly box, I would pick a size 8, as that size is a great overall representation of a large Golden Stonefly nymph. Due to size limitations in materials, I typically tie the Shimmer Stone in size 4 to 10. D-Rib is just too large to tie with in sizes smaller than a 10. When it comes to larger variations, I have had to switch to different hook manufacturers to find a similar-style hook in the larger sizes, so if you want to make larger flies, you'll have to adjust accordingly.

My go-to rig for fishing the Shimmer Stone is usually as a point fly in a two-fly indicator nymph-style set up. Due to the fly's size, I like to tie 4X or heavier tippet to the eye of these flies, as they may twist up your leader from time to time, and because they are usually fished deep along the bottom of the stream. My rule of thumb is to fish with the heaviest tippet that still allows me to successfully fool fish without sacrificing flies to a vicious strike or snag on the bottom.

If I decide to tie a dropper off of a Shimmer Stone, I prefer to tie the tippet to the eye of the fly as opposed to the bend of the hook, as it seems to tangle the tippet about the tails and antennae less frequently this way. I prefer my droppers a little

Trout will eat Golden Stonefly nymphs pretty much any time of the year, as this brown trout did in March on a New England stream. During high water, Golden Stonefly nymphs become available in the drift and trout will habitually eat them.

longer than most and usually space the flies anywhere from 18 to 24 inches from one another depending on depth and current speed. If the water is deeper or more turbulent, then I space them out closer to 24 inches than 18. I like to run my leader on average anywhere from $7^{1}/_{2}$ feet to 10 or more feet overall, but I will adjust accordingly depending on the conditions.

On any given outing, when I decide to fish a pair of Shimmer Stones under an indicator I'll always tie the larger of the

The Dimmer Stone is a more natural version of the Shimmer Stone that uses mottled Thin Skin for the back of the fly.

two flies on first and then tie the smaller one on the dropper section below. This not only makes for a more streamlined set up, but it also helps you turn the rig over when casting, as everything from the indicator to the split shot, from the lead fly down to the dropper fly, is tapered and will have less frequent tangles.

Longer rods in the $9^{1}/_{2}$- to 10-foot range in 4-, 5-, or 6-weight configurations seem to be the best choices from my experiences, especially when faced with larger rivers, windy conditions, and large fish. More often than not when fishing with nymphs in the size ranges I mentioned, I turn to a 10-foot, fast-action rod, as it will handle a pair of large Shimmer Stones, added weight, and a large indicator over a wide range of conditions. The larger, faster action rod will also aid in line management and mending.

Over the years I have found that the Shimmer Stone can be fished as a dropper under a large dry fly as well. A large, buoyant dry fly built out of foam like the Busted Stone or any of the other options out there will suffice. The dry fly needs to be large enough and buoyant enough so as to not sink from the weight of the Shimmer Stone. Due to the larger size of the two flies needed, you'll want to open up your casting loops slightly to prevent tangles. Over the past few seasons the Shimmer Stone has had several variations on the original Golden Stone color scheme. Diverse species of fish, including trout, steelhead, and smallmouth bass, have fallen victim to this pattern over the last five years, and it has earned a permanent space in several anglers' fly boxes. Today, I tie the Shimmer Stone in golden, brown, black, and olive, with the first two shades being the best for trout. A tungsten-beaded version has also been a hot fly for those who like to fish with heavier anchors in a European nymphing rig, and I always have a few tied in this manner for my own fly boxes.

Variations

The standard Shimmer Stone is a moderately weighted stonefly, but you can make it much heavier by adding a tungsten bead or lead wire. If having a variety of weighted flies is something you strive for, going up or down a size on the tungsten bead, changing the diameter of the wire, or both will give you many options for various depths and current speeds. Some of the competitive anglers will even use different colors of Datum Glo Brite for hot spots to decipher the weights of the patterns in their fly boxes. For this particular pattern, I personally have not used any sort of hot spots on them due to the size of the imitation, but I have heard from other anglers that they like hot spots in chartreuse for the golden variation and hot orange for the brown.

I tie a more muted variation of this fly by omitting the flashy back and replacing it with a strip of mottled Thin Skin. The tying steps are the same, just change the shellback, and when I tie the fly in this manner, it's called a "Dimmer Stone," as it isn't bright and flashy.

GOLDEN SHIMMER STONE

Hook:	#6-10 Tiemco 2302
Bead:	Copper, size to match; tungsten bead optional
Tail/Antennae:	Ginger Hareline Life Flex
Underbody:	Lead-free wire (.020"–.025") covered with yellow Uni-Stretch
Thread:	Yellow 140-denier Ultra Thread
Abdomen:	Brown Hareline Flashyback under light Golden Stone Hareline D-Rib (medium)
Thorax:	Golden Stone Hareline Hare-Tron Dubbin
Legs:	March Brown Brahma hen
Wing Case:	Brown Hareline Flashyback

Note: You can substitute the Tiemco 2312 or the Daiichi 1260 for the hook.

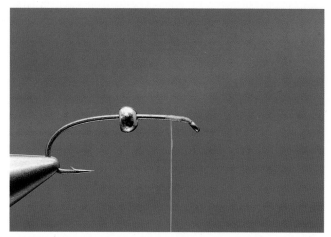

1. Slide a bead on the hook and affix the hook in the vise. Like the Infant Stone, slide the bead rearward and attach the tying thread with six to eight turns, starting at the eye.

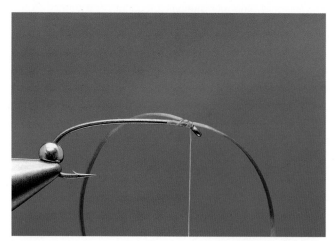

2. Cut a straight section of Life Flex from a hank, and tie it in the middle to the front of the hook with three to four thread wraps working back toward the eye.

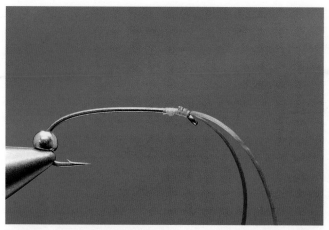

3. While keeping steady tension on the thread, fold the other section of Life Flex over the front of the hook, wrap the thread rearward with steady tension, and then whip-finish the thread. Keep the thread wraps to a minimum or else you will not be able to slide the bead back forward to the hook eye.

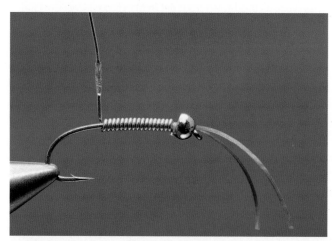

4. Trim the antennae so that they are the length of the hook, and push the bead back forward to the eye. Take a section of lead-free wire, and begin wrapping it rearward from one turn behind the eye. When you reach the hook point, use a pair of flat pliers, and compress the end of the wire to create a taper in the underbody. A drop of superglue on the hook shank before adding the wire will help in preventing the wire from rolling.

26. Repeat steps 21 and 22, dub another noodle of Hare-Tron Dubbin, and wrap it on the hook covering the thread wraps. Make sure you make this second section half the size of the space you have left to tie on.

27. Tie in another section of Brahma hen for the second section of legs. Be sure to fold the tip of the feather rearward and wrap the thread over the tips.

28. Fold the Flashyback forward again, secure it with three to four turns of thread, fold it rearward again, and wrap your thread another five or six turns over the material so that the thread hangs against the second section of dubbing you just wrapped. Half hitch the thread so that it will not unravel.

29. Dub a third noodle of Hare-Tron Dubbin to the thread, and wrap it around the hook to make the final thoracic section of the fly.

30. Tie in the third and final section of Brahma hen in the same manner of the first two pairs. Fold the feather rearward after three or four turns of thread, and secure the butt ends with thread wraps, then trim the feather away.

31. Twist a fine noodle of Hare-Tron Dubbin to the thread, and wrap it over the butt ends of the Brahma hen. Use only enough to complete one turn of dubbing around the fly.

32. Pull the Flashyback forward over the top of the front of the fly, and secure it in place with two or three wraps of thread.

33. Fold the Flashyback rearward over the back of the fly. Leave a small section of the material forward over the top of the bead of the fly. This will leave a section for the head of the fly making four distinct sections on the thoracic region.

34. Trim the excess Flashyback from the fly, and complete a four-turn whip-finish with your thread. Cement the thread wraps, and then coat the Flashyback with a thin layer of epoxy or Clear Cure Goo Thin to add durability to the wing case.

35. Invert the fly in the vise, and take note of the distinct segmentation from the D-Rib and the lighter colored underbody. Take a piece of velcro or a comb, and brush out the fibers to either side of the fly.

36. The combed out sections of Antron and hare's ear from the thorax make up the gills of the fly.

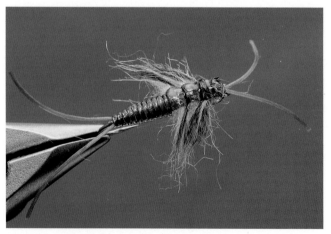

37. Notice the distinct segmentation and pronounced thoracic regions reminiscent of the natural.

BROWN SHIMMER STONE

Hook: #6-10 Tiemco 2302
Bead: Copper, size to match; tungsten bead optional
Tail/Antennae: Brown Hareline Life Flex
Underbody: Lead-free wire (.20"–.25") covered with brown Uni-Stretch
Thread: Rusty brown 140-denier Ultra Thread
Abdomen: Brown Hareline Flashyback under light Golden Stone Hareline D-Rib (medium)
Thorax: Seal brown Hareline Hare-Tron Dubbin
Legs: March Brown Brahma hen
Wing Case: Brown Hareline Flashyback

Note: You can substitute the Tiemco 2312 or the Daiichi 1260 for the hook.

OLIVE SHIMMER STONE

Hook: #6-10 Tiemco 2302
Bead: Brass, size to match; tungsten bead optional
Tail/Antennae: Olive Hareline Life Flex
Underbody: Lead-free wire (.20"–.25") covered with olive Uni-Stretch
Thread: Olive 140-denier Ultra Thread
Abdomen: Peacock Hareline Flashyback under olive Hareline D-Rib (medium)
Thorax: Olive Hareline Hare-Tron Dubbin
Legs: Golden straw Brahma hen
Wing Case: Peacock Hareline Flashyback

Note: You can substitute the Tiemco 2312 or the Daiichi 1260 for the hook.

BLACK SHIMMER STONE

Hook: #6-10 Tiemco 2302
Bead: Black, size to match; tungsten bead optional
Tail/Antennae: Black Hareline Life Flex
Underbody: Lead-free wire (.20"–.25") covered with black Uni-Stretch
Thread: Black 140-denier Ultra Thread
Abdomen: Black Hareline Flashyback under olive Hareline D-Rib (medium)
Thorax: Black Hareline Hare-Tron Dubbin
Legs: Golden straw Brahma hen
Wing Case: Black Hareline Flashyback

Note: You can substitute the Tiemco 2312 or the Daiichi 1260 for the hook.

PART III
Streamers

CHAPTER 17

Designing Streamers

In the last ten to fifteen years, there has been an absolute explosion in streamer fishing. From technological advances by rod companies, to groundbreaking advances in fly lines, to the explosion and refinement of articulation in streamers, to the variety of new techniques used for fishing them, to the advent of cutting-edge synthetic materials, we are in a bit of a Renaissance in the world of streamer fishing. It is an exciting time, and streamer fishing is no longer a game solely based upon a slowly swung fly fished on a tight line through runs. Actively retrieved flies have built-in movement and fish-enticing actions

Big, expansive rivers are some of the best places to fish streamers, especially when the rivers are swollen. Fishing streamers from a drift boat is one of the most exciting and effective ways to employ those types of flies.

Angler Mike Schmidt showing that even mid-size trout will thump an articulated streamer.

reminiscent of many of the top lures fished in the gear world, and they have created a following of anglers whose mantra is "The tug is the drug." I'll readily admit that I'm an obsessed streamer fisherman to the core. Out of all the ways that I have fished with flies, streamer fishing is by far one of the most exciting.

The aggressive nature of streamer fishing is the "dirty" side of the sport that appeals to an ever-growing demographic of anglers. If you like to chase big fish, enjoy the sight of an aggressive fish inflicting pain on your fly, or strive for that next arm-wrenching strike from a voracious predator, then streamer fishing will definitely scratch that itch. There isn't a day that goes by where I don't envision a large brown trout or voracious northern pike putting a hurt on a streamer that I am working through a piece of water. Whether you are imagining that next super-realistic baitfish pattern, or dreaming up something that will behave a certain way in the water, there's a loose blueprint you should follow when building streamers. Whatever it is you have in mind, and wherever you intend to fish your fly, there are certain attributes that I have found are paramount in building a solid pattern. A well-designed streamer doesn't happen by accident: it's the result of a delib-

erate process that often requires a bit of time and effort on paper, at the vise, and on the water.

Like insect imitations, streamers can be broken down into two distinct categories: realistic imitations and suggestive/attractor patterns. From my personal experiences, the latter are often better than the former for a variety of reasons. Realistic streamer patterns often lack the natural, inherent movement that comes from materials like fox fur, marabou, and rabbit. In my opinion, having materials that convey movement is more important than any other attribute of streamer design. The streamers that I tie and fish regularly are meant to be actively fished, whether you manipulate them aggressively via hard strips of the line or jerks of the rod tip through the water column, or whether you hop and skip them up and down off the stream bottom. They are all built out of materials that, when not actively retrieved by the angler, will freely move and undulate with the current. Although realistic streamer patterns look fantastic in hand, many times due to their enhanced realism, their materials are rigid and lifeless in the water.

Everything has a time and a place, and sometimes more realistic streamers will work better than attractor patterns. But this is more the exception than the rule when dealing with trout

To put the size of this fish in perspective, this particular brown fell for a 5¹/₂-inch Headbanger Sculpin. When fishing streamers on medium to large rivers, be sure to have an adequate net.

not always be possible, and the Hog Snare streamer in a later chapter is an example of a pattern that can take a bit of time to tie, especially on the first attempt. But as is the case with the Snare, sometimes good things take time, and if the pattern proves to be effective, then the time spent at the vise was well worth it in my book.

I'm a firm believer that streamer patterns designed with color variety are generally more effective than those that are solid in color. The next time you're out fishing, take a close look at one of the fish you catch—study the skin of a brown trout, for example. That fish's skin probably has more hues than you think. A close inspection will reveal that a brown trout has shades of red, white, purple, yellow, aquamarine, and even orange and black all on the same fish. The fish's color patterns are complex, not simple, and so is just about everything else in nature. Although solid-colored streamers work well at times, I believe that multi-colored imitations are more often successful, as they better represent the living organisms that fish see on a daily basis. If you want to catch trout and other species under all conditions with streamers, you need to experiment with color combinations.

I don't think streamers are only an option when the water is high and off-color; I fish them under all conditions. It's a type of hunting, and once you are committed, you observe the conditions and formulate the best plan of attack for those conditions. This may require you to have a few extra pieces of gear, and a few more varieties of streamers in your box to cover different situations. As when I'm tying and fishing nymphs, I like to break my streamers down into categories. The three cate-

gories that I use for my patterns (aside from realistic and suggestive) are weighted, unweighted, and transitional streamers.

Weighted streamers are those that I typically will fish on a floating line with a stout, virtually stretch-free leader design. I fish these flies when the stream conditions are optimal, clear and low, and when I want to fish directly on the bottom of the river. This particular style of streamer fishing is the best under those circumstances, as it is the most stealthy, and it will still afford the angler the opportunity to fish streamers when most would opt to fish insect imitations. This is also a viable option when fish are hanging a little deeper in structure and you need your fly to get down quickly. Many of the weighted streamers that I tie and fish are not just confined to being fished on floating lines, though; you can also try them on an integrated sinking line.

Unweighted streamers are movement-rich designs with no additional weight added. These flies hover in the water column and are best fished on an integrated sinking line, as the line will be the means by which the fly gets to different levels of the water column. These flies are built to be fished primarily in the upper portion of the water column, even when fished on a sinking line, as they are neutrally buoyant designs that will have exceptional movement in the horizontal and vertical planes of the water column as a result of action imparted by the angler.

Transitional streamers are those that incorporate a mix of the two designs listed above. They have lots of movement incorporated into their design with minimal amounts of weight in their construction. This subtle combination gives the angler a fly that can be fished in a variety of ways and water types and throughout the water column. Transitional streamers fill the void between the bottom-oriented streamers and those that are fished in the upper portion of the water column.

You will soon see that many of the streamers I tie fit into one of these three categories. Some patterns, with a slight modification, can fit into all three, but for the most part, they all are meant to be employed in a specific part of the water column. Having a variety of streamers from all three of these categories will vastly improve your game with streamer fishing. To increase your success even more, carry a variety of color combinations as well.

The best piece of advice I can give you is this: carry only one large box on the river when wading with maybe one or two of each pattern's colors. This will give you the room to have a full complement of various streamer patterns in your box on hand rather than just twelve of the same pattern in different colors. You will quickly learn that a dozen of the same fly will limit your fly selection, as these patterns eat up the most space in the largest of fly boxes. Variety is key. If you're on foot, you can always keep more flies nearby in your vehicle in case you run out of that magic fly pattern. If you're fishing from a drift boat you'd better have a few more flies in the boat with you, but for the most part when wading, it's better to have a variety of patterns than just a few patterns in a variety of colors.

sizes and color combos until you find what seems to be the most effective, and then build your assortment from there. Make sure to have some weighted and unweighted variations in that assortment, as this will allow you to cover a wider variety of depths in the river you're fishing.

Weight can be added in a variety of ways: lead or lead-free wire to the hook shank in the underbody of the pattern, various types of dumbbell eyes, or a combination of the two. I suggest having a couple of different weights for each of your favorite color combinations, as a lightly weighted or moderately weighted version with one that is unweighted will cover most of your situations nicely.

I suggest using hooks that run anywhere from 3X to 4X in length, as once you get into some of the larger shanked streamer hooks, they can work as a keel with larger fish once hooked, forcing the hook out of the fish's jaw. I also think the pattern flows a little better on those sizes of hooks as well, and that once you get into long 6X to 10X streamer hooks, the profile isn't as appealing.

Personally, I prefer natural color tones for the Bloody Baitfish, but I will from time to time carry some wildcard colors for specific situations. When I'm going to be fishing high, dirty water, I stick with dark colors, like a solid black or brown, or colors like white, yellow, or chartreuse, as they are also more visible in the water column under those conditions. I will also tie a few in multi-tone configurations. For instance, under high, dirty water I have a lot of faith in black over chartreuse, as this combination has worked really well in those conditions for brown trout.

With the wide variety of colors available in rabbit strips these days, the color combination possibilities are vast. Aside from the natural colors, you have single-color dyed variations, multi-color dyed variations, barred variations, and more. To add a little more mottling to the fly design, you could also get creative in the tail construction. By taking two different colors of marabou plumes and palmering them together, you can give a nice mottled effect to the tail of the fly, similar to the tail on a Headbanger Sculpin. At the end of the day, the Bloody Baitfish is a relatively simple streamer pattern that, with a little practice, can be tied in under five minutes. Because it is so effective and takes so little time to tie, it is a viable pattern for any fly box.

CHINCHILLA BLOODY BAITFISH

Hook:	#1/0-6 Partridge Universal Predator
Thread:	Gray-brown 140-denier Ultra Thread
Eyes:	Angel Clear Cure Goo Molded Eyes ($^3/_{16}$")
Tail:	White marabou
Body:	Pearl Flat Diamond Braid
Rib:	Red Ultra Wire (medium)
Wing:	Chinchilla rabbit strip ($^1/_8$")
Belly:	Pearl Ice Dub
Gills:	Red Ice Dub

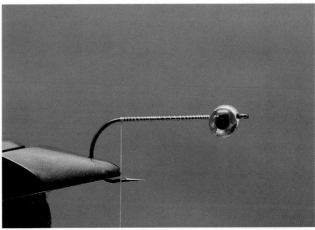

1. Start the tying thread behind the hook eye, and advance it rearward approximately two eye lengths. Attach your dumbbell eyes of choice to the underside of the hook using a figure-eight method of tying. Place a drop of superglue or Zap-A-Gap on the thread wraps on the top and bottom of the dumbbell eyes, then advance the thread to the barb of the fly.

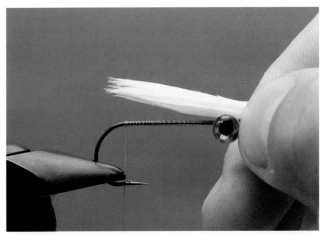

2. Align the tips of a pair of marabou plumes, and wet them on your sponge. Measure the two plumes of marabou to the shank of the hook to get your length. The tail should be approximately the length of the hook.

3. Begin wrapping the tying thread in open spiral-wraps over the marabou plumes, making sure to keep them on the top of the hook.

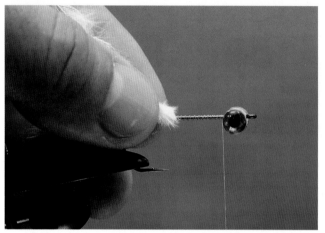

4. While maintaining tension on the tying thread, lift up the marabou plumes and advance the tying thread down the hook shank to a point just behind the dumbbell eyes.

5. Release the marabou and wrap over it with two or three turns of thread. This additional step will ensure that the underbody is uniform when wrapping the Diamond Braid.

6. Wrap the thread rearward, covering the butt ends of the marabou and making sure that it is all covered. Take your section of red Ultra Wire, and make two loose wraps over it at the base of the marabou tail.

7. Secure the wire to the top side of the hook, working the thread toward the dumbbell eyes and back to the base of the tail.

8. Preen the fibers of the rabbit strip in either direction to expose the hide. If you have to, wet your fingers, as it will make this step easier to accomplish.

9. Take four turns of thread, each progressively tighter, over the bare hide on the rabbit strip. Once you have completed those turns while maintaining tension on the thread, pull the rabbit strip back and advance the thread to a point just behind the dumbbell eyes.

10. Lift up the tail portion of the rabbit strip with a double-edged razor, and cut the hide so that the rabbit strip is a little longer than the marabou tail.

11. Pull the rabbit strip back over the vise with either a piece of wire or a small hair clip, and clip it to the jaws. This will keep the material out of your way as you tie the remaining steps of the fly.

12. Affix a section of flat Diamond Braid to the top of the hook with three or four turns of thread.

13. Pull the flat Diamond Braid rearward to pull the butt ends under the tying thread, and continue wrapping the thread rearward to the base of the wing. Then, wrap forward again to the dumbbell eyes.

14. Wind the flat Diamond Braid forward in tight, consecutive, slightly overlapping wraps. This will ensure that there are no gaps in the body as you complete the body. Tie the material off behind the dumbbell eyes, half hitch the thread, and clip the excess Diamond Braid.

15. Release the rabbit strip from the hair clip, and begin winding the wire over the thread wraps, securing the rabbit strip to the fly. It should take roughly three to four turns of wire to accomplish this.

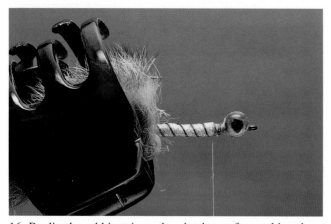

16. Reclip the rabbit strip to the vise jaws after making those first few turns of wire. Advance the rib in front of the wing, and make a series of open spiral-wraps to the dumbbell eyes of the fly. Once completed, either invert the fly in the vise or turn it upside down using the rotary function.

17. Grab a small clump of pearl Ice Dub, and pull the fibers apart in your hand, repositioning the material to form an even bunch of fibers. Place the bunch on the underside of the fly, and take two turns of thread over the middle of the bundle.

18. While keeping constant tension on the thread, preen the Ice Dub rearward toward the tail, being mindful of the hook point. Once you have teased the fibers rearward, advance the thread in front of the bunch and wrap a few turns of thread followed by a half hitch to prevent the clump from coming undone. It is also a viable option to run a turn or two of thread on top of the front of the bundle.

19. Repeat the previous two steps again in front of the last bundle. Tie in a clump of Ice Dub in the middle of the clump, tease it rearward, and advance the thread.

20. Remove a clump of red Ice Dub from the package, and tease the fibers in your hand, realigning the material to get the maximum amount of length out of it. The red will be used for the gills, so use about half as much as you used in each of the prior clumps of pearl Ice Dub.

21. As with the pearl Ice Dub, use thread tension and tease the fibers rearward. You should be right at the base of the dumbbell eyes on this step.

22. Tie in a third and final clump of Ice Dub in the same manner as the last three clumps. Make sure you leave yourself roughly an eye's length of space behind the eye so that you can tie the rabbit strip wing down to the hook correctly. The last thing you want to do is crowd the eye, preventing yourself from running the tippet through the hook eye.

23. As seen from the top, the Ice Dub belly will flare to either side of the hook when it is tied correctly. You can also tease the fibers by gently pulling downward on them. If you overdress the belly section, you can also brush the belly with a comb or piece of velcro to remove the excess. Be sure to start your thread close to the base of the dumbbell eyes for the next step.

24. Pull the rabbit wing forward over the top of the fly so that it seats flat and tightly across the top. You can add a drop of Loctite gel to the top of the fly prior to doing so if you prefer. Take four or five relatively tight turns of thread over the rabbit strip wing.

25. Trim the hide from the front of the hook, and continue wrapping the thread over the butt end of the rabbit strip, building a neatly tapered thread head. Once satisfied, whip-finish, cut the thread, and cement the thread wraps with your cement of choice.

TAN BLOODY BAITFISH

Hook:	#1/0-6 Partridge Universal Predator
Thread:	Tan 140-denier Ultra Thread
Eyes:	Steel Clear Cure Goo Molded Eyes ($^3/_{16}$")
Tail:	White marabou
Body:	Pearl Flat Diamond Braid
Rib:	Red Ultra Wire (medium)
Wing:	Tan or light brown rabbit strip ($^1/_8$")
Belly:	Pearl Ice Dub
Gills:	Red Ice Dub

OLIVE BLOODY BAITFISH

Hook:	#1/0-6 Partridge Universal Predator
Thread:	Olive 140-denier Ultra Thread
Eyes:	Smoke Clear Cure Goo Molded Eyes ($^3/_{16}$")
Tail:	White marabou
Body:	Pearl Flat Diamond Braid
Rib:	Red Ultra Wire (medium)
Wing:	Olive variant rabbit strip ($^1/_8$")
Belly:	Pearl Ice Dub
Gills:	Red Ice Dub

WHITE BLOODY BAITFISH

Hook: #1/0-6 Partridge Universal Predator
Thread: White 140-denier Ultra Thread
Eyes: Angel Clear Cure Goo Molded Eyes (^{3}/16")
Tail: White marabou
Body: Pearl Flat Diamond Braid
Rib: Red Ultra Wire (medium)
Wing: White rabbit strip (^{1}/8")
Belly: Pearl Ice Dub
Gills: Red Ice Dub

BROWN BLOODY BAITFISH

Hook: #1/0-6 Partridge Universal Predator
Thread: Dark brown 140-denier Ultra Thread
Eyes: Steel Clear Cure Goo Molded Eyes (^{3}/16")
Tail: White marabou
Body: Pearl Flat Diamond Braid
Rib: Red Ultra Wire (medium)
Wing: Chocolate brown rabbit strip (^{1}/8")
Belly: Pearl Ice Dub
Gills: Red Ice Dub

BLACK BLOODY BAITFISH

Hook: #1/0-6 Partridge Universal Predator
Thread: Black 140-denier Ultra Thread
Eyes: Lava Clear Cure Goo Molded Eyes (^{3}/16")
Tail: White marabou
Body: Pearl Flat Diamond Braid
Rib: Red Ultra Wire (medium)
Wing: Black rabbit strip (^{1}/8")
Belly: Pearl Ice Dub
Gills: Red Ice Dub

YELLOW BLOODY BAITFISH

Hook: #1/0-6 Partridge Universal Predator
Thread: Yellow 140-denier Ultra Thread
Eyes: Lava Clear Cure Goo Molded Eyes (^{3}/16")
Tail: White marabou
Body: Pearl Flat Diamond Braid
Rib: Red Ultra Wire (medium)
Wing: Yellow rabbit strip (^{1}/8")
Belly: Pearl Ice Dub
Gills: Red Ice Dub

CHAPTER 19

Ice Pick

For decades, the Zonker streamer has been a staple in the boxes of fly fishermen across the globe. The original pattern, created by Dan Byford of Colorado, has seen a slew of variations over the years and has spawned a tying style that, nearly forty years later, we still associate with the original pattern. Today, when we discuss any sort of streamer tied with a rabbit strip, we call it a "Zonker," and we can thank Mr. Byford for this innovation.

I have always been fond of the Zonker and of the many variations that I've used over the years. Rabbit hair has great movement and is available in a wide selection of sizes and colors.

Large trout, even rainbows, often cannot resist a large meal that a streamer can provide, as is evident by this large Colorado rainbow trout who hammered a ginger colored Ice Pick. LANDON MAYER

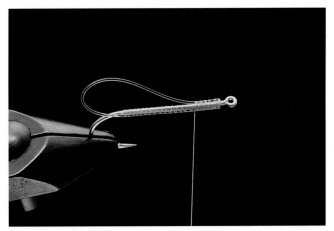

4. Fold the other end of the mono, and kink the rear, making sure to match the butt ends at the front of the hook. Begin wrapping the thread over both sections of the mono as you work your way rearward toward the loop.

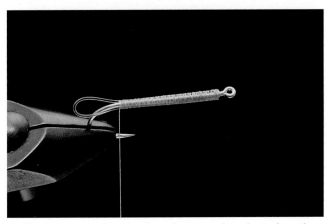

5. Continue wrapping the thread rearward to the point where the hook bend starts. To ensure the loop doesn't move around, you can run a second course of thread forward and back to the rear using a little more thread tension. You can apply a thin coat of superglue or Zap-A-Gap, but this isn't necessary.

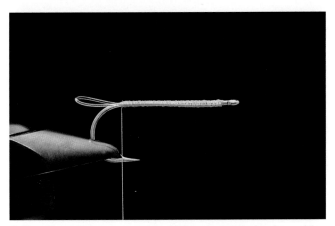

6. Note how the mono runs parallel to the hook shank on either side. The loop serves two purposes: to cut down on the longer tail from fouling and to provide a wider foundation on which to affix the wing to the fly.

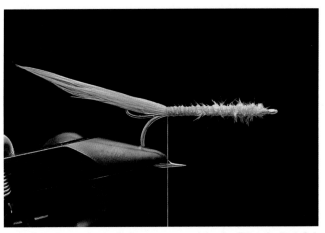

7. Using the same technique you used in the Bloody Baitfish (see page 137), select a pair of marabou plumes, align the tips, and wet them with your sponge. Measure the marabou against the hook, and tie them in the same manner as the Bloody Baitfish. Trim the butt ends near the hook eye and return the thread to the rear of the fly.

8. Preen the hair from the rabbit strip with your fingers, exposing the bare hide, and secure the strip to the top of the hook with four tight turns of thread. Advance the thread in front of the rabbit strip, and half hitch the thread. Lift up the strip over the marabou, and trim it with a double-edged razor. Trim the hide of the tail section just inside the tips of the marabou. The hair from the rabbit strip will lay rearward past the marabou. The longer tail will give the fly more swimming action in the rear.

9. Fold the rabbit wing rearward, and using a hairclip, clip it to the jaws of the vise to keep it out of your way. Take one brush from a package of EP Sparkle Brushes, and secure the brush to the hook shank. If you've got a half-used section of brush, trim some of the flashy material from either side of the stainless steel wire. This will help affix the brush to the fly. Run a course of thread over the wire to a point just behind the hook eye.

10. In a series of open spiraled wraps, begin wrapping the Sparkle Brush forward. The wraps should be roughly ⅛ inch apart as you work your way forward down the hook. These particular brushes are fairly dense, so you do not need to wrap them tightly. Once you reach the hook eye, tie the brush off and trim the wire with an old pair of scissors or wire cutters.

11. Comb the fibers downward from either side of the fly with your brush. This will allow you to affix the rabbit strip wing to the hook.

12. After combing the Sparkle Brush down and rearward, remove the rabbit strip from the hair clip, and pull it forward over the top of the fly. Separate the rabbit hair with your fingers, and secure the wing to the front of the hook with two to three turns of thread.

13. Trim the front of the rabbit strip with your scissors, wrap another five or six turns of thread over the butt end of the rabbit strip hide, and half hitch the thread. Remove a small bundle of Laser Dub from the package, pull it apart, and align it in your hand. Once it's aligned, secure the bundle in the center with two turns of thread so that it's directly on top of the thread head of the fly.

get more length from it as well. The tail, although soft, has more underfur and guard hairs and maintains its shape better than the body fur because it has a tendency to collapse and shrink in size when wet. I was looking to create a wing of Arctic fox that was three-dimensional, encompassing the upper half of the fly—similar to the mallard flank feather on the Zoo Cougar. If I could make a wing similar in nature, it would act like a parachute, aiding in the fly's ability to remain neutrally buoyant in the water column.

After some trial and error, it dawned on me while I was looking at one of Bob Popovics' fly patterns. Bob pioneered reverse-tied bucktail patterns as a way to not only create the illusion of size and depth with minimal material, but also to create extreme durability in the fly. In the end, this little trick not only made the Arctic fox tail wing durable, it also aided in fanning the fibers out 180 degrees across the top of the hook shank, which was essentially the idea I had in mind.

Like all of the articulated streamers that I tie, I opted for the standard connection of Beadalon 19 Strand in .018-inch diameter coupled with a pair of 3D ProEye lure-making beads. Friend and fellow tier Mike Schmidt first introduced me to these beads, and I have used them in all of my articulated flies since. I like the colors and sheen that 3D ProEye beads give the fly and their ability to reflect light. What they also do (that standard glass beads will not) is maintain a consistent diameter in the body of your fly, which is important when it comes to the look of the fly. This is more of a personal preference, but for me, it really makes the connections flow much more fluidly.

For the front of the fly, I added dumbbell eyes to the underside of the front hook to give the fly some movement in the vertical plane, similar to a jig. The more movement, the better. I wanted a fly that had all kinds of triggers and movement, and the Hog Snare ended up with just that.

Fishing

Due to this particular fly's size, I have found that the pattern is best fished on an a 7 or 8-weight rod with an integrated sinking line and a shorter, stout leader. When I say stout, I mean a butt section of 35- to 40-pound mono tapered down to 15-pound mono to the fly, with overall leader lengths of 2 to 5 feet. A stiff saltwater mono tapered leader will aid in turnover and help with laying the fly out straight. Instant contact with your fly is paramount, as the fly will often get smashed by a fish the second it lands. I also found that this fly really shines when you manipulate it more erratically in the water column. For example, Kelly Galloup's jerk-strip retrieve is an excellent method to manipulate this fly. The pause in the middle of the retrieve is usually when the fly gets hammered. This pause, coupled with the materials—even with the weighted dumbbell eyes—causes the fly to hover in the water column and undulate, giving off the illusion of life, which seems to be irresistible to the fish. Often, when other streamers get a refusal, the Hog Snare will still get eaten as result of these attributes.

Due to the fly's size, this particular pattern has been a true big-fish magnet for me in the last couple of years, taking sev-

Angler and guide Dan Harrison holds an impressive brown trout that fell victim to a variation of the Hog Snare. CAMERON CHIOFFI

eral fish in the high 20-inch mark. Aside from trout, this fly has proved its worth with a variety of other species, including northern pike, tiger muskie, muskie, smallmouth bass, largemouth bass, pickerel, and walleye, making the Hog Snare a multi-species fish catcher.

Variations

Like many of the flies I tie, the Hog Snare has evolved as a result of angler needs, some custom requests, and other obstacles I encountered. The first and most noteworthy variation was making a smaller version of the pattern. After years of fishing the pattern, I realized that I needed a slightly smaller version of the fly in the mix. I devised a double that was roughly $4^{1}/_{2}$ to $5^{1}/_{2}$ inches long by simply omitting the middle articulated shank from the fly. The nice thing about the smaller version is that you can easily toss it on a 6-weight rod. To reduce the weight of the fly, I later changed the lead dumbbell eyes to a lighter version made out of an alloy with an epoxy eyeball. When these eyes are incorporated in the original three-part design, it can actually be cast on a 6-weight with a slightly open casting loop. In a pinch, this is beneficial, as many anglers aren't accustomed to fishing for trout with a 7- or 8-weight rod. I have also made a few variations with clear Fish Masks in place of the dumbbell eyes to make a virtually weightless, large-profiled streamer. By doing this, you get maximum movement and erratic behavior when fished on an integrated sinking line.

If I know that the Hog Snares I'm tying are going to be fished primarily for large, toothy fish like pike, I will use a size 2/0 or 1/0 hook in the front and a size 1 in the rear, coupled with a larger diameter Beadalon 49 Strand rather than the 19 for added durability. The only caveat is that you had better hand-pick your fox tails, because if they are not long enough, the pattern will be disproportionate. Whatever colors you decide upon, fish them with confidence.

OLIVE AND YELLOW HOG SNARE

Rear Hook:	#1 Gamakatsu SP11-3L3H or Partridge Universal Predator
Thread:	Olive 140-denier Ultra Thread
Tail:	Olive Holographic Flashabou under yellow schlappen fluff under olive marabou
Body:	Olive Cactus Chenille (medium)
Hackle:	Yellow schlappen
Mottling:	Barred olive/green flake Crazy Legs
Wing:	Olive Arctic fox tail
Shank:	Fish-Skull Articulated Shank (35 mm)
Underbody:	Lead-free wire (.020")
Rear Collar:	Olive Holographic Flashabou under yellow schlappen fluff
Body:	Olive Cactus Chenille (medium)
Hackle:	Yellow schlappen
Mottling:	Barred olive/green flake Crazy Legs
Wing:	Olive Arctic fox tail
Connection:	Beadalon 19 Strand stringing wire (.018") with 2 Irish Janns Netcraft ProEye 3D lure beads
Front Hook:	#1/0 Gamakatsu B10S or #1 Partridge Absolute Predator
Rear Collar:	Olive Holographic Flashabou under yellow schlappen fluff
Body:	Olive Cactus Chenille (medium)
Hackle:	Yellow schlappen
Mottling:	Barred olive/green flake Crazy Legs
Wing:	Olive Arctic fox tail
Collar:	Light olive Senyo Laser Dub
Head:	Yellow Senyo Laser Dub
Eyes:	Dumbbell eyes or red Psuedo Eyes

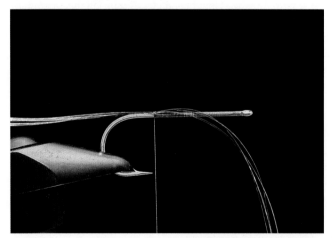

1. Place your rear hook in the vise, and begin the tying thread directly behind the hook eye. Continue wrapping thread to the hook point, and tie in four strands of Holographic Flashabou in the middle with two turns of thread.

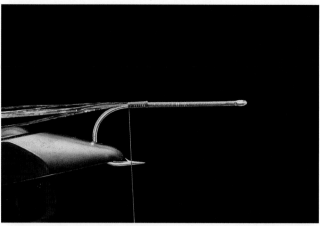

2. While maintaining tension on the thread, fold the forward bundle of Flashabou rearward over the top of the fly and continue wrapping the thread to the point where the bend of the hook starts.

3. Tie the lower end, or shorter schlappen feather, by the tips. Advance the tying thread about a third of the way down the hook shank.

4. Wrap the schlappen feather forward to the tying thread, and tie it off with two or three wraps in front of and behind the feather. Reverse the thread rearward back toward the barb of the hook to slant the feather rearward.

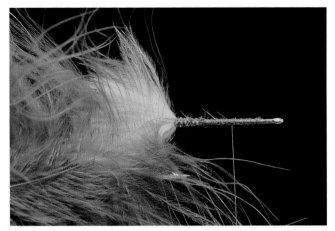

5. Select a thin-stemmed marabou plume from a bag of marabou. Tie the plume in by the tips with several turns of thread. Advance the thread to the halfway point of the hook.

8. Select a schlappen feather and a section of Cactus Chenille, and tie the two in at the rear of the fly, right at the base of the marabou. The schlappen should be under the Cactus Chenille. Pull the fibers out from the last $1/2$ inch of the Cactus Chenille to reduce bulk and aid in securing the material to the hook.

6. Wrap the marabou plume forward in consecutive wraps toward the tying thread. Tease the fibers from the feather with your fingers after every turn to release any trapped fibers.

9. Continue wrapping the thread forward to a point one eye length behind the eye.

7. Tie off the end of the plume with three turns over the top of the feather and in front of the feather. Trim the stem and wrap the thread rearward over the fibers to make the marabou lay rearward over the schlappen and Flashabou. The thread should stop at the hook point so as to keep some mass in the tail.

10. Wrap the Cactus Chenille forward in close wraps to the point where the tying thread is hanging. Take two turns over the top of the chenille and two turns in front. While maintaining tension on the thread, trim the chenille, leaving a $1/4$-inch section of excess. Pull the flashy material from the chenille, exposing the thread core.

11. Bind down the exposed chenille core with the tying thread, making a neat thread head, and half hitch. Begin palmering the schlappen feather forward toward the hook eye in even and open wraps, teasing the fibers rearward on every turn.

12. Palmer the schlappen to the hook eye, and secure the feather with thread wraps. Trim the feather at the stem and wrap over the butt ends.

13. Tie a pair of Crazy Legs in the middle on top of the hook with two turns of thread. Pull one Crazy Leg to the near side, and the other to the far side of the hook. Wrap a couple more turns of thread, fold the forward sections rearward, wrap your thread back to the base of the schlappen, and half hitch.

14. Cut a section of hair from an Arctic fox tail roughly the diameter of a pen. Cut the hair as close to the hide as possible to get the maximum length. Be sure to choose hair that has adequate length, or else the wing will not be long enough.

15. Hold the fox hair firmly between your thumb and pointer finger and comb out the underfur with a flea comb. By cleaning out the shorter underfur, you reduce the chance of the hair falling out or rolling around the hook after being tied.

16. While keeping the bundle of fox hair tips aligned, transfer the bundle to your thread hand and tie it in reverse, with the butt ends rearward and the tips over the front of the hook. Use your opposite hand to take three turns of thread over the butt ends.

17. While maintaining constant and steady tension on the thread, keep the fox hair affixed to the top of the hook and cover the butt ends of the hair. Return the thread to the base of the schlappen.

18. With your opposite hand, grab the entire bundle of hair and pull it rearward over the top of the fly.

19. Take three to four turns of thread over the hair, creating a bullet head, while also fanning the hair out 180 degrees across the top of the fly. Make a half hitch in the thread, and then complete the section with a four-turn whip-finish. Cement the thread wraps with a coat of Clear Cure Goo Hydro.

20. Notice how the fox hair flairs out to either side of the hook giving the fly more dimension, similar to that of the mallard flank feather in Kelly Galloup's Zoo Cougar.

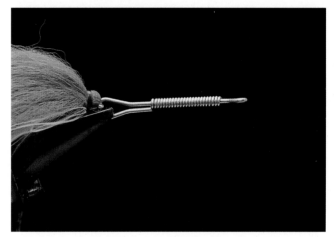

21. Slide a 35-millimeter Articulated Shank through the eye of the rear hook. Affix the connection in the jaws of your vise, put a thin layer of superglue on the shank, and wrap a layer of .025-inch lead-free wire to the connection. To prevent any mishaps, use your hairclip, and clamp the rear hook to the jaws of the vise.

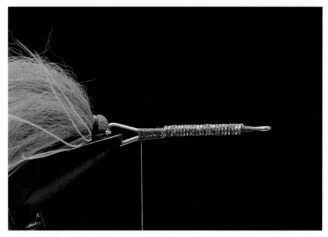

22. Attach the tying thread behind the eye of the shank, and work your way rearward, closing the rear clasp of the shank with the thread.

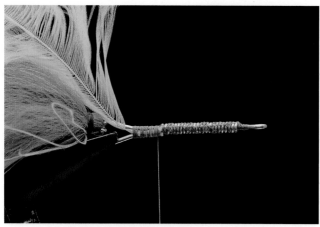

23. Preen the fibers of another shorter schlappen feather rearward, trim the tip section, and tie it in by the tip of the feather.

24. As you did in the tail, take four to five turns of the feather forward, teasing the fibers rearward on every turn. Tie off the feather, and wrap back over the base of the feather toward the rear of the shank to force the fibers rearward. The feather should take up that rear section behind the lead-free wire.

25. Tie two strands of Flashabou in the top of the shank with two to three turns of thread.

26. While maintaining tension on the thread, pull one half of each of the two strands to the near side of the shank and the other half to the far side, and secure them with thread wraps.

27. Tie in another schlappen feather with a section of Cactus Chenille on top of it at the base of the schlappen connection. Be sure that the schlappen feather for this section is larger than the one used in the tail.

28. As you did in the tail, advance the thread to eye, wrap the Cactus Chenille, and tie it off behind the eye. Then, palmer the schlappen feather through the Cactus Chenille, and tie it off as well.

29. As you did in the tail, tie in a pair of Crazy Legs by the middle, affix one to each side of the shank, fold the legs rearward, and build a thread head for the next step.

30. As you did in the tail, remove a long section of Arctic fox tail the same size as the first bundle, remove the underfur with a comb, and reverse-tie the bundle to the front of the shank. After several turns of thread, fold the hair rearward, and tie over the front of the bundle, forming a bullet head. Whip-finish and cement the thread wraps.

31. Cut a 3½-inch section of Beadalon 19 Strand stringing wire (.018 inch), and run it through the eye of the shank. Pull hard on the wire to kink it slightly, then add a pair of beads to the wire and set it aside.

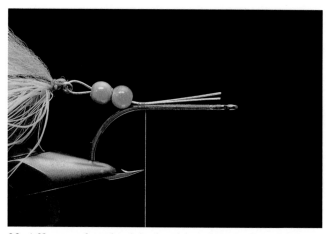

32. Affix your front hook in the vise and start a layer of thread from the hook eye to the bend of the hook. Manipulate the wire from the rear two sections so that they lie side by side. Affix the wire to the top of the hook shank with four turns of thread, leaving a bead's space between the rear bead and shank eye, and between the front bead and the rear of the front hook.

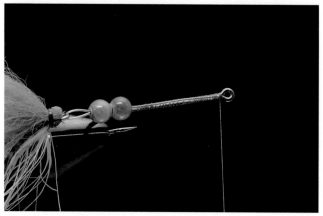

33. While maintaining the sections of Beadalon alongside one another and on top of the hook, continue winding the thread forward, covering the butt ends.

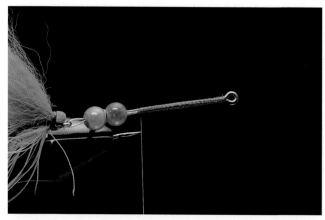

34. Continue winding the thread to the rear of the hook with increasing tension, then forward to the hook eye and back to the rear again. Each course should be wrapped slightly tighter than the last, following with a half hitch.

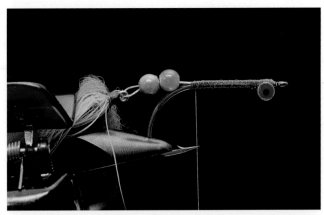

35. Advance the thread to a position roughly two eyes' distance behind the eye, and begin figure-eight tying the dumbbell eyes to the underside of the hook. Place a small drop of Zap-A-Gap or superglue on the top and underside of the dumbbell eyes, and return the thread to the rear.

36. As you did for the shank, tie in a shorter section of the base of a schlappen feather by the tip, wind the feather forward four or five turns, tie off and wrap the thread rearward to the hook point, and half hitch.

37. Affix two pieces of holographic Flashabou in the middle to the near side of the hook, fold the other half to the far side of the hook, and continue the thread back to the base of the schlappen.

38. Attach a schlappen feather by the tips with a section of Cactus Chenille on top of it, and work the thread forward to about a hook eye's distance behind the dumbbell eyes. Be sure to use the largest schlappen feather of the three for this section of the fly, as you want to build a progressively larger taper as you near the head.

39. As you did earlier, wind the Cactus Chenille forward to the thread, secure the chenille, and trim away the excess. Palmer the schlappen forward through the Cactus Chenille and tie off the feather, also trimming away the excess.

40. Cut a pair of barred Crazy Legs, and affix them to the top of the fly by the middle with two turns of thread. Pull one to the near side, the other to the far side, and secure them with a couple of turns of thread before folding them rearward and returning the thread to the base of the schlappen.

41. As you did earlier in the tail and center of this fly, take a longer section of Arctic fox tail the same size as the first two bundles, remove the underfur with a comb, and reverse-tie the bundle to the hook behind the dumbbell eyes. After several turns of thread, fold the hair rearward and tie over the front of the bundle, forming a bullet head.

42. Remove two even bundles of light olive Laser Dub from the package, and manipulate the fibers in your hand to get the maximum length out of them. Take the two bundles, and tie them in by the middle on both the top and bottom of the fly with two turns of thread. The top bundle should be right on top of the bullet formed by the Arctic fox, and the bottom bundle should be directly under it on the other side.

43. While maintaining constant tension, advance the thread in front of the two bundles, while teasing the two bundles rearward with your opposite hand.

44. Take five or six turns of thread in front of the bundle, and half hitch the thread so that it won't unravel.

45. Brush out the collar on all four sides with your flea comb to remove any loose fibers and help spread the Laser Dub around the fly 360 degrees.

46. The collar should look like this after being brushed out.

47. Remove a generous bundle of yellow Laser Dub from the package, manipulate the fibers in your hand to maximize length, then tie the bundle in at the middle with two turns of thread, keeping the bundle on the top of the hook.

48. While maintaining tension on the thread, advance it in front of the bundle while teasing the Laser Dub rearward. Take two turns in front of the bundle and half hitch the thread.

49. Invert the fly and complete the same process on the underside of the fly. While holding the bundle in your opposite hand and maintaining thread tension, complete the same process as you did in the last step.

50. After advancing your thread in front of both bundles and half hitching your thread, brush out the loose fibers with your flea comb.

51. Continue this process, working your way to the eye of the hook. Attach a bundle of Laser Dub to the top of the fly, then the bottom, comb it out, and continue on. This process may take three or four revolutions before you can pull the Laser Dub head rearward and whip-finish and cement your thread.

52. Brush out the fibers in the entire head area so that they make a 360-degree revolution around the head.

53. Begin trimming the head to shape with a pair of synthetic-specific scissors, starting with the two sides of the dumbbell eyes. Reach into the side of the fly, seat the edge of your scissors along the dumbbell eyes, and trim the sides flat.

54. After trimming the sides, trim the top of the head at an angle, being sure to round the edges as you trim it away.

55. After completing the top of the fly to your liking, do the same for the bottom of the head. The size of the head is entirely up to you, but personally, I like to make the head similar in size to a Muddler Minnow.

56. The three-section version is a handful and comes in at roughly 6$\frac{1}{2}$ to 7 inches long. To make the smaller two-section fly, just omit the center shank and tie the connection as instructed.

TAN AND YELLOW HOG SNARE

Rear Hook:	#1 Gamakatsu SP11-3L3H or Partridge Universal Predator
Thread:	Tan 140-denier Ultra Thread
Tail:	Yellow Holographic Flashabou under yellow schlappen fluff under tan marabou
Body:	Root beer Cactus Chenille (medium)
Hackle:	Yellow schlappen
Mottling:	Barred golden yellow/pearl flake Crazy Legs
Wing:	Dark tan Arctic fox tail
Shank:	Fish-Skull Articulated Shank (35 mm)
Underbody:	Lead-free wire (.020")
Rear Collar:	Yellow Holographic Flashabou under yellow schlappen fluff
Body:	Root beer Cactus Chenille (medium)
Hackle:	Yellow schlappen
Mottling:	Barred golden yellow/pearl flake Crazy Legs
Wing:	Dark tan Arctic fox tail
Connection:	Beadalon 19 Strand stringing wire (.018") with 2 Rusty Nail Janns Netcraft ProEye 3D lure beads
Front Hook:	#1/0 Gamakatsu B10S or #1 Partridge Absolute Predator
Rear Collar:	Yellow Holographic Flashabou under yellow schlappen fluff
Body:	Root beer Cactus Chenille (medium)
Hackle:	Yellow schlappen
Mottling:	Barred golden yellow/pearl flake Crazy Legs
Wing:	Dark tan Arctic fox tail
Collar:	Dark tan Senyo Laser Dub
Head:	Dark tan Senyo Laser Dub
Eyes:	Chartreuse Psuedo Eyes (medium)

BLACK AND PURPLE HOG SNARE

Rear Hook:	#1 Gamakatsu SP11-3L3H or Partridge Universal Predator
Thread:	Black 140-denier Ultra Thread
Tail:	Purple Holographic Flashabou under purple schlappen fluff under black marabou
Body:	Black Cactus Chenille (medium)
Hackle:	Purple schlappen
Mottling:	Black/purple Hot Tipped Crazy Legs
Wing:	Black Arctic fox tail
Shank:	Fish-Skull Articulated Shank (35 mm)
Underbody:	Lead-free wire (.020")
Rear Collar:	Purple Holographic Flashabou under purple schlappen fluff
Body:	Black Cactus Chenille (medium)
Hackle:	Purple schlappen
Mottling:	Black/purple Hot Tipped Crazy Legs
Wing:	Black Arctic fox tail
Connection:	Beadalon 19 Strand stringing wire (.018") with 2 Purple Haze Janns Netcraft ProEye 3D lure beads
Front Hook:	#1/0 Gamakatsu B10S or #1 Partridge Absolute Predator.
Rear Collar:	Purple Holographic Flashabou under purple schlappen fluff
Body:	Black Cactus Chenille (medium)
Hackle:	Purple schlappen
Mottling:	Black/purple Hot Tipped Crazy Legs
Wing:	Black Arctic fox tail
Collar:	Black Senyo Laser Dub
Head:	Black Senyo Laser Dub
Eyes:	Chartreuse Psuedo Eyes (medium)

GRAY AND WHITE HOG SNARE

RUSTY BROWN HOG SNARE

Rear Hook:	#1 Gamakatsu SP11-3L3H or Partridge Universal Predator
Thread:	White 140-denier Ultra Thread
Tail:	Pink Holographic Flashabou under white schlappen fluff under gray marabou
Body:	Pearl Cactus Chenille (medium)
Hackle:	White schlappen
Mottling:	Barred clear/pearl flake Crazy Legs
Wing:	Gray Arctic fox tail
Shank:	Fish-Skull Articulated Shank (35 mm)
Underbody:	Lead-free wire (.020")
Rear Collar:	Pink Holographic Flashabou under white schlappen fluff
Body:	Pearl Cactus Chenille (medium)
Hackle:	White schlappen
Mottling:	Barred clear/pearl flake Crazy Legs
Wing:	Gray Arctic fox tail
Connection:	Beadalon 19 Strand stringing wire (.018:) with 2 Arctic Ice Janns Netcraft ProEye 3D lure beads
Front Hook:	#1/0 Gamakatsu B10S or #1 Partridge Absolute Predator
Rear Collar:	Pink Holographic Flashabou under white schlappen fluff
Body:	Pearl Cactus Chenille (medium)
Hackle:	White schlappen
Mottling:	Barred clear/pearl flake Crazy Legs
Wing:	Gray Arctic fox tail
Collar:	Silver minnow belly Senyo Laser Dub
Head:	Silver minnow belly Senyo Laser Dub
Eyes:	Chartreuse Psuedo Eyes (medium)

Rear Hook:	#1 Gamakatsu SP11-3L3H or Partridge Universal Predator
Thread:	Rusty brown 140-denier Ultra Thread
Tail:	Brown Holographic Flashabou under fiery brown schlappen fluff under brown marabou
Body:	Root beer Cactus Chenille (medium)
Hackle:	Fiery brown schlappen
Mottling:	Barred golden yellow/pearl flake Crazy Legs
Wing:	Fiery brown Arctic fox tail
Shank:	Fish-Skull Articulated Shank (35 mm)
Underbody:	Lead-free wire (.020")
Rear Collar:	Brown Holographic Flashabou under fiery brown schlappen fluff
Body:	Root beer Cactus Chenille (medium)
Hackle:	Fiery brown schlappen
Mottling:	Barred golden yellow/pearl flake Crazy Legs
Wing:	Fiery brown Arctic fox tail
Connection:	Beadalon 19 Strand stringing wire (.018") with 2 Rusty Nail Janns Netcraft ProEye 3D lure beads
Front Hook:	#1/0 Gamakatsu B10S or #1 Partridge Absolute Predator
Rear Collar:	Brown Holographic Flashabou under fiery brown schlappen fluff
Body:	Root beer Cactus Chenille (medium)
Hackle:	Fiery brown schlappen
Mottling:	Barred golden yellow/pearl flake Crazy Legs
Wing:	Fiery brown Arctic fox tail
Collar:	Sculpin olive Senyo Laser Dub
Head:	Sculpin olive Senyo Laser Dub
Eyes:	Chartreuse Psuedo Eyes (medium)

Alternative design using the Fish Mask in place of the dumbbell eyes. This fly is virtually weightless and can be cast on a lighter weight fly rod.

CHAPTER 22

Headbanger Sculpin

Sculpins are some of my favorite baitfish to replicate, and for years I was constantly refining a few patterns as newer materials became available. In streams where sculpins and trout reside together, they are a major source of food for larger trout. Whenever present, fly imitations of sculpins will consistently work better than other types of streamers. If I had to pick only one style of streamer to fish, it would easily be the sculpin. Every season, my largest trout of the year are taken on sculpin imitations. Even in watersheds where sculpins are not present, trout will readily fall victim to a well-presented sculpin pattern, as the trout instinctively recognize them as easy prey due to their

Sculpins are bottom dwelling forage fish that lack a swim bladder. They are poor swimmers and move erratically in short darting movements making them easy meals for motivated trout.

Using weighted streamers on a floating line in lower water conditions is an often-overlooked tactic for catching big, aggressive trout. This particular brown trout ate a Headbanger Sculpin during flows far less than what is normal for this particular stream.

limited ability to swim. Because of their physical makeup and lack of a swim bladder, sculpins are not strong swimmers, and they typically dart in short bursts off the streambed. These attributes make them a favorable food source for trout. It behooves fly anglers fishing with sculpin imitations to impart similar action to their flies when fishing imitations of the creatures.

Sculpins are fascinating creatures if you look at them closely. They are bottom-dwelling fish that do not have a swim bladder, are streamlined in shape, and possess a large, bulbous head with winglike pectoral fins protruding from their sides. They are typically mottled in appearance and are generally found in shades of black, olive, brown, tan or a combination of the like. Sculpins, like many other fish, will take on the color of the river bottom they inhabit and use this as camouflage from predators. They typically range from 1 to 4 inches in length, with some larger specimens, but for the most part, this is an ideal size range for even a smaller trout to ingest.

Active retrieves that mimic the movements of a real sculpin will inevitably draw more positive responses from the fish. Although many anglers don't fish their imitations directly on the bottom, they could exponentially increase their success by

doing so. If you look at sculpin imitations, several resemble the fish itself, but due to their material composition, do not actually reach the bottom of the stream.

Let's take the Muddler Minnow, for example, since it's probably the most widely recognized streamer pattern that is essentially a sculpin imitation. The head and collar are made out of spun deer hair, which is buoyant, and so the fly will not immediately descend to the river bottom even when fished on a heavy sinking line. Often, Muddlers and similar imitations never come close to the river bottom, but are still effective patterns. One can only assume that the action they have in the water and their acoustic footprint are what make them such consistent producers. But, what I have found, is that when you take that same pattern, add weight to the design, and fish it close to or directly on the bottom with short strips followed by exaggerated pauses, the pattern will be an even deadlier imitation.

The sculpin imitation I had in mind to build would have to embody several key elements. I needed materials that would give the impression of life, would sink quickly to the bottom, and would also be able to remain near or on the bottom when fished. As you may know, many materials tiers use to create lifelike moving patterns will collapse once wet, quickly losing the dimension they possess when dry.

For years I remembered reading about the Goby Snap Heads by Roman Moser. I knew that a broad, counterbalanced, weighted head would be the perfect ingredient for building the bottom-oriented sculpin that I had envisioned. The only caveat for me was that, although Roman's Goby Heads were similar to what I had in mind, they weren't cost-effective from a production fly tier's perspective. I ran through many possible alternatives, including tungsten cones, beads, and Cross-Eyed Cones. What I found was that each alternative had limitations and just didn't make the type of head that I was looking to build into the fly. The biggest problem was that those weights never keeled the fly so that it would ride point-up as it bounced along the bottom.

In 2011 The Flymen Fishing Company introduced a new product to the fly-tying market that solved my problem. The Fish-Skull Sculpin Helmet, although similar to Moser's Goby Snap Heads, had a slightly different profile, was constructed of a metal alloy instead of tungsten, and was also built to act like a keel, allowing a fly to ride in the point-up hook position as long as you put the heavier side on the top of the shank, or in reverse. Approximately 70 percent of the Helmets' weight is situated below the shank of the hook. This heavily weighted bottom acts in the same manner as a dumbbell on a fly, which will help keep the fly down in the current and near or on the bottom.

This pattern was one of the few that came to fruition quickly. I had received some sample packages of the Helmets in the mail, and a few hours later, I had an idea. Many of the sculpin patterns that were popping up in all of the tying circles on the Internet were all similar in nature. Collars of rabbit fur with tails and bodies made of rabbit strip seemed to be the favorite—simple and effective for sure, but not what I had in mind.

Personally, I wasn't satisfied with the appearance those particular flies took on once wet. Although I use rabbit hair frequently for its lifelike movement, it has one major drawback. Rabbit fur is not a long hair, and most rabbit fur is, on average, an inch long. The sculpin I had envisioned was to be articulated and roughly 4 to 5 inches inches long. Rabbit fur was just not long enough. For a larger pattern, the proportions would not be remotely close to what I had envisioned if I used rabbit strips.

In the previous chapter, I wrote about the Hog Snare streamer and the use of reverse-tied Arctic fox tail to create a three-dimensional, 180-degree wing about the top of the fly. I quickly recognized that the Hog Snare, with some minor alterations and additions, could make a fabulous bottom-oriented sculpin imitation. The Hog Snare was already one of my most effective larger articulated flies, so converting the pattern to a bottom-oriented sculpin was an obvious choice.

I think a streamer pattern that uses a lot of flashy material in its construction can often be a deterrent on the river, as fish will quickly realize it is a fake under normal stream conditions. My goal was to design a pattern that would have applications across the spectrum of water conditions, not just high and dirty water. To go hand in hand with these ideals, the Northeast was once again experiencing a long period of droughtlike conditions, so fishing with an integrated sinking line was almost entirely out of the question. A stealthier approach using a floating line and a weighted fly was much more reasonable, so I figured the sculpin I envisioned would be an ideal pattern for these conditions.

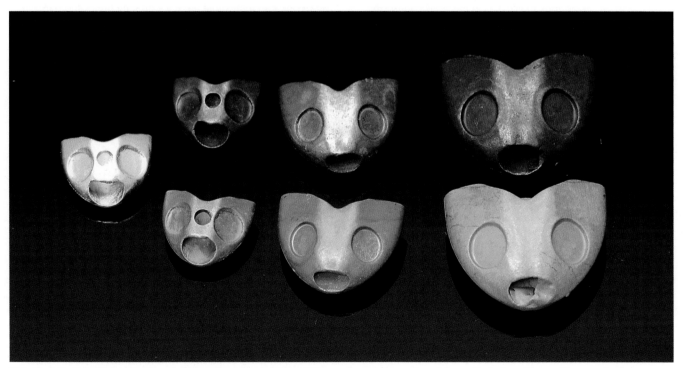

Fish-Skull Sculpin Helmets come in three sizes. From left to right are the mini, small, and large. Both the olive and brown shades come in all three sizes, with the mini also available in silver, as seen in this picture.

The first thing that changed from the Hog Snare design was the tail. Rather than just palmering one marabou plume around the fluff of a schlappen feather, I wanted something a little more dense, but with multiple colors. I settled on two marabou plumes palmered together, and in varied colors. The first color I attempted was dark olive, as the majority of sculpins in my home waters were predominantly an olive or black hue. To create a mottled tail, I decided on pairing two marabou plumes of different colors together. I used the same materials in the connection area of the articulation, and it made the fly flow nicely.

The rest of the body of the fly used the same materials as the Hog Snare: Cactus Chenille wrapped to just behind the eye of the hook with a schlappen feather palmered through the body, a pair of barred Crazy Legs on either side to provide a little more mottling and movement in the fly, and a reverse-tied wing of Arctic fox tail. The only difference this time was I rotated the wing 180 degrees from the position I tied it in. In other words, the wing was tied in on the underside of the shank of the hook because I was envisioning an inverted fly that tracked with its hook points up.

A rear view of a large Sculpin Helmet shows that there is more material on the bottom of the head. Notice the thicker diameter of the metal on the bottom, which aids in the keeling effect this product has on patterns, working much like inverted jigs.

Not all marabou plumes are created equal. It pays off in the long run to inspect and separate the usable plumes from a package. Look for plumes that are full with long fibers and thin, pliable stems.

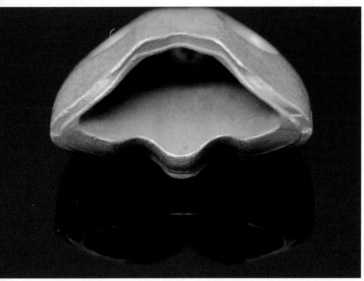

A frontal view of a large Sculpin Helmet with eyes already affixed in the recessed eye wells. Whenever tying these flies in quantity, it saves time to tie certain sections first. In this case, affixing the eyes with a drop of gel Loctite Super Glue before tying the fly is a way to save time.

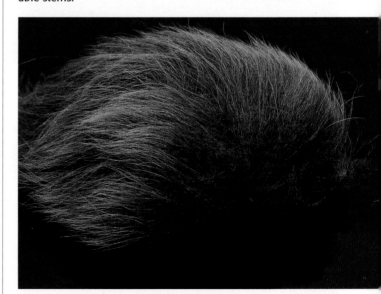

Arctic fox tail is a great material for streamer patterns. Although it has excellent movement in the water, it is made up of more guard hairs, unlike Arctic fox body hair, which is much softer. The additional guard hairs make the hair a bit coarser, which helps your fly maintain its profile when wet.

Fishing

That next morning I hit the stream early with a handful of my new patterns. It was mid-July and the beginning to a hot and humid week. As I mentioned earlier, the rivers were low, and the folks who controlled the releases were conserving water with flows extremely low. The river was a skeleton: approximately one-third to one-half of the streambed was exposed, so the fish were concentrated in places with good gradient and some depth. The major pools were 2 to 3 feet shallower than normal, which made for wary fish, even more than usual on this heavily pressured tailwater.

I fish the Headbanger in the same manner as the Cellar Dweller—a cast upstream into the head of a run or boulder strewn section allowing the fly to sink to the bottom before imparting any action works exceptionally well. Often, I will let the fly roll the bottom on the first couple of casts through a particular piece of water before actively retrieving the fly, as many fish will eat the fly as it dead drifts along the bottom.

In the past when fishing with a floating line and weighted streamers, I planned my approach to each piece of water I was going to fish in the same manner: from downstream, working my way up. I can't tell you how many times I've heard from other anglers that big streamers, or streamers in general, are not effective in low, clear conditions. I beg to differ. On this partic-

ular morning, with extra low clear water, the Headbanger Sculpin had its first glimpses of greatness. In a three-hour session on the water, I brought to hand eleven browns from 17 to 22 inches long. The takes were aggressive and sometimes outright vicious, with cartwheeling browns going airborne after being hooked. Some of the fish even gave chase into the shallows before inhaling the fly.

Over the course of the next six months, this particular retrieve under a variety of conditions proved deadly, and accounted for numerous fish over 20 inches, and even a handful just shy of the 30-inch mark. I also learned that slowly rolling the bottom of the river similar to a dead-drifting nymph will entice wary fish into eating the fly; this has been a viable technique when other methods of presentation are unsuccessful, and will also work in the dead of winter when trout can be less inclined to chase a fly (see page 162 in the Cellar Dweller chapter).

Most standard monofilament leader material was elastic and often lead to several lost fish after trying to set the hook. My typical leader of choice ran from $4\frac{1}{2}$ feet to roughly 9 feet. The butt section was typically constructed of 30- to 40-pound-test, tapering down to 12- to 15-pound-test. The aforementioned problem with setting the hook was encountered on leaders in excess of 6 feet, as the longer the leader, the more one had to strip-set to send the hook point home due to the amount of stretch throughout the length of the material.

Often brown trout will occupy sections of the river that are shallow and may not require a sinking line. Angler Pat Burke fooled this particular brown in a shallow section of water. PAT BURKE

Elastic leader material was also problematic because it was too supple, making it difficult for many anglers to turn over a heavier fly. Fishing a fly of this nature is not a high-line-speed, tight-looped affair. If you don't open your cast, the fly will collapse your leader in a messy pile, or jettison off your rod, risking severe damage to the blank or even worse, breaking the blank.

One day while ordering trout leaders and fluorocarbon, I picked up a few spools of RIO Alloy Hard Saltwater Mono Tippet, hoping to solve this particular problem. When they arrived, I quickly pulled a section of tippet off one of the spools and gave it a good pull in my hands. Immediately, I realized that I had found my solution. For the next few weeks, I spent time on the water breaking in my new leaders made of this material, and

I found that the number of fish I dropped on the hook set went down dramatically. As long as I stayed tight to the fly without slack in the system as I retrieved line, I was confident that I would hook and land a majority of the fish that I felt strike the fly or that I saw move the end of the fly line. I now build all of my leaders for streamer fishing in this manner with that material, regardless of what kind of line I'm using.

I also learned, in employing this type of pattern, the importance of fishing with a weight-forward floating line. Weight-forward lines have a larger, more aggressive taper at the end of the line, and many distance casters and anglers use them to turn over larger flies. What I found was, although I could push my 6-weight rod into delivering heavier patterns, a fast-action 7- or 8-weight of 9 feet or longer was the perfect set up, as it

A family of olive/black Headbanger Sculpins. On top, from left to right, is the mega, which is roughly 7 to 7¹/₂ inches with double articulations (two hooks and three sections); then the standard articulated, which is roughly 5 to 5¹/₂ inches long with two hooks. The bottom row depicts the mini Headbanger using all three sizes of heads. Left to right is the small, then the mini, and finally the large Helmet. These flies cover a wide spectrum of species, from small native brook trout all the way up to large migratory bull trout in the Pacific Northwest.

not only could handle the added weight and size of the fly, but it also drastically cut down on fatigue when casting all day.

To be honest, although using a floating line with the Headbanger is my preferred method, many different retrieves have produced fish, and this fly works well on an integrated sinking line too. Be willing to vary your retrieve, presentation, or line type when your success rate is lacking. I later learned throughout the course of a year that this particular pattern was effective under a variety of conditions. For the last three seasons, I have taken fish on this pattern all twelve months of the year in the Northeast, and it's not just a trout pattern, either. This Headbanger Sculpin is a deadly streamer pattern for smallmouth and largemouth bass, northern pike, and even steelhead.

Variations

Many fly anglers, especially trout fishers, are intimidated by large streamers. The first variation that spawned from the original Headbanger Sculpin was the direct result of many of my fly customers requesting a single-hooked version of the pattern. To be honest, this variation was a no-brainer and easy to accomplish with a minor change in the hook style.

The single-hook version is a great smaller sculpin pattern if you find that the larger pattern isn't getting the attention you're after. I typically tie it with the mini and small Helmets on a size 2 or 4 hook, but I have also used and sold many with the large Helmet and larger irons. The single-hook version is a versatile pattern, as I have often used it as an anchor in a Euro nymphing–style setup or as a lead fly under an indicator. Sometimes, a sculpin dead-drifted through a run is an effective technique and will also produce quality trout.

Later, I was approached by some fly fishermen in the Pacific Northwest who targeted bull trout. They requested larger versions of the Headbanger Sculpin. A simple solution to these requests was to add a 35-millimeter shanked section in between both hooks, much along the lines of my Hog Snare pattern. By adding the shank to the middle of the fly, I gained the added size I was looking for and upped the overall size of the fly to 7 inches or more based upon the quality of the marabou I had on hand. The first few batches I sent out West did well, and I got some great feedback from those that were fishing them. Because the water they were fishing in was pretty heavy, I added several turns of .030-inch lead wire to the middle shank portion and the front hook to aid in getting this fly to the bottom quickly.

In the beginning I only tied the Headbanger in a couple of colors, mostly combinations reminiscent of what was found in nature: shades of olive, black, tan, or brown. In time, I began experimenting with more colors, some bright, as I had a feeling from past experiences they would work well. Today, I have found that the Headbanger Sculpin can be altered in color and size to whatever your heart desires. Some of my favorite color combinations, aside from earth tones, are brown and yellow, black and red, olive and yellow, and black and chartreuse. Experiment often, and find the colors that you have confidence in.

OLIVE AND BLACK HEADBANGER SCULPIN

Rear Hook:	#2 Gamakatsu SP11-3L3H or Partridge Universal Predator
Thread:	Olive-brown 140-denier Ultra Thread
Tail:	Black Holographic Flashabou under one black and one olive marabou plume
Body:	Olive Cactus Chenille (medium)
Hackle:	Black schlappen
Mottling:	Barred olive/green flake Crazy Legs
Wing:	Dark olive Arctic fox tail
Connection:	Beadalon 19 Strand stringing wire (.018") with 2 Split Pea Janns Netcraft ProEye 3D lure beads
Front Hook:	#1 Gamakatsu B10S or #2 Partridge Absolute Predator
Rear Collar:	Black Holographic Flashabou over one black and one olive marabou plume
Body:	Olive Cactus Chenille (medium)
Hackle:	Black schlappen
Mottling:	Barred olive/green flake Crazy Legs
Wing:	Dark olive Arctic fox tail
Pectoral Fins:	Olive Senyo Laser Dub
Head:	Olive Fish-Skull Sculpin Helmet (large)

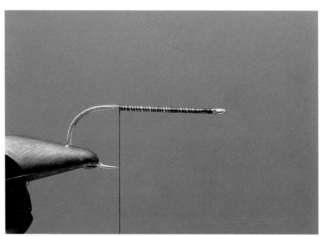

1. Place your rear hook in the vise. Start the thread behind the eye, and run a course of thread to a point in line with the hook point.

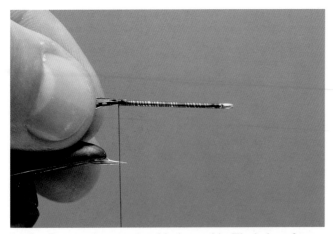

2. Cut five or six strands of holographic Flashabou from a hank and tie them in the middle with two to three turns of thread on the top of the hook. Fold the forward-facing strands of Flashabou rearward, maintaining tension on the thread, then wrap over the Flashabou to the rear of the hook where the bend starts.

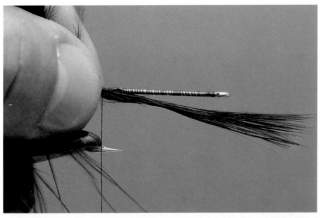

3. Align one olive and one black marabou plume by the tip of the feathers. Try to pick feathers that are of similar size and length. With the tips aligned, wet them with a sponge and tie them in to the hook shank. The addition of water helps keep the fibers together as you affix them to the hook.

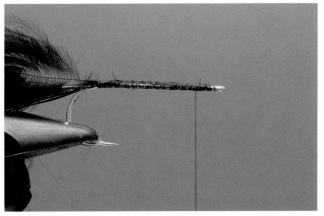

4. Cover the butt ends of the marabou plumes with wraps of thread, and advance the thread forward to a point behind the eye.

5. Grab the stems of the two marabou plumes, and wind them together simultaneously down the hook shank. To ensure none of the fibers become trapped, tease the fibers rearward with every turn on the hook.

6. Secure the marabou plumes with three turns of thread in front of and behind the stem. To add durability to the tail, wrap the thread over the marabou plumes, working your way back to a point roughly halfway between the hook point and barb, then add a half hitch to the thread.

7. The body is similar to the body of the Hog Snare (see page 184). Take one black schlappen feather, tease the fibers rearward, and trim the tip. Take a section of olive Cactus Chenille (medium), and place it on top of the schlappen feather. Tie the two in by the tips at the base of the marabou tail. Take your hair clip and clamp the schlappen feather to the jaws of the vise.

8. Advance the tying thread forward to the eye, and wind the Cactus Chenille forward to the hook eye. Tie off the chenille and trim the extra. Be sure to remove the fibers from the thread core in the same manner that you did for the Hog Snare.

9. Begin winding the schlappen feather forward using even and open wraps. Tease the fibers on the feather rearward on every turn as you work your way toward the hook eye.

10. Wind the schlappen feather to the tying thread, and secure the feather with three turns in front of and behind the feather before trimming. After securing the feather, build a uniform thread base the size of the hook eye, located directly behind the eye.

11. Remove two barred Crazy Legs from a hank, and tie them in on top of the hook in the middle with two turns of thread.

12. While maintaining tension on the tying thread, pull one leg to the near side of the hook and the other to the far side of the hook.

13. Continue winding the thread in between the Crazy Legs, and return the thread to the rear of the wraps. Fold the forward-facing Crazy Legs rearward, and secure them with three to four turns of thread, then add a half hitch.

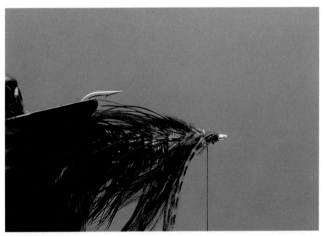

14. Invert the hook in the vise, making sure that the thread is in the rearmost position of the thread head.

15. Remove a pencil-size section from an Arctic fox tail, being sure beforehand that the bundle has adequate length. The key is to select a section that, when tied in reverse, will reach the base of the tail of the fly.

16. Remove the underfur from the bundle of Arctic fox tail with a flea comb.

17. As you did in the Hog Snare, you're going to reverse-tie the wing on this fly, only this time you'll invert the wing to the underside of the hook shank. While holding the bundle with your opposite hand, begin winding thread wraps over the butt ends of the fox tail with the fibers facing forward over the hook eye.

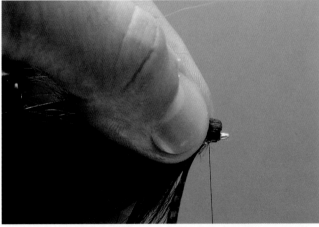

18. Being careful not to impale your thumb and pointer finger on the hook point, pull the wing rearward over the hook point, forming a bullet head. Begin winding the thread over the bundle of Arctic fox fur with three or four turns.

19. After making your initial turns of thread over the bundle, put a half hitch in the thread, then follow that with a four-turn whip-finish, trim the thread, and coat the thread wraps with your cement of choice. I like to use Clear Cure Goo Hydro.

20. Cut a 3½-inch section of Beadalon 19 Strand stringing wire (.018-inch) from a spool with your wire cutters, and thread it through the eye of the hook, pulling gently on the end to kink the wire. Thread two Split Pea 3D ProEye Beads to the wire and set aside.

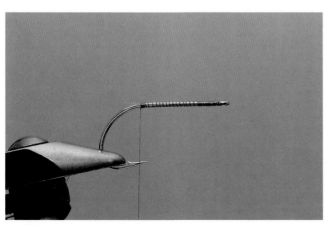

21. Place your front hook in the vise, and wind the tying thread rearward, starting directly behind the eye and ending at the point where the hook bend begins.

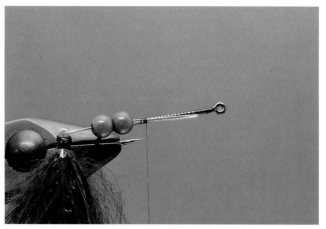

22. Affix the rear section of the fly to the top of the hook in the vise with three or four turns of thread. Be sure to tie the section in on top of the hook with the two sections of wire side-by-side.

23. Wind the thread forward to the hook eye, covering all of the wire and the butt ends, then reverse the thread with slightly more tension, and return to the rear. Take a second course of thread forward to the eye and back to the tie-in point of the wire, keeping a steady amount of increasing tension on the thread without breaking it.

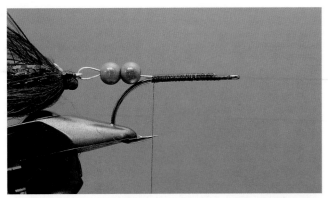

24. After affixing the rear section, return the fly to the upright position. This is a glimpse at the connection correctly tied. Be sure when you affix the tail that both hook points are in the same position, as you can easily tie the tail in upside down. Clamp the rear section to the jaws of your vise with your hair clip to avoid any injuries.

25. As you did in the tail of the rear section of the fly, take one olive and one black marabou plume, tie them in by the tips, and advance the thread to the midway point of the hook.

26. Wind the two marabou plumes around the hook simultaneously, teasing the fibers out so they aren't trapped after each turn. After making four or five turns, secure the plumes with the tying thread, cut the stems, and return the thread rearward over the plumes, forcing them to lay backward. The thread should be hanging in line with the point of the hook.

27. Trim three to four pieces of black Holographic Flashabou from a hank, and secure them in the middle of the bunch to the near side of the hook. While maintaining tension on the thread, fold the front of the bundle over the top of the hook to the far side and secure the Flashabou with three or four more turns of thread, ending at the base of the marabou collar.

28. Similar to the rear section, only using a larger feather, secure a schlappen feather by the tip to the hook with a section of olive Cactus Chenille on top of it. Advance the thread forward to a point roughly at the one-third point of the hook shank.

29. Wind the Cactus Chenille forward to the thread, and secure the chenille with three turns of thread in front of and behind it. Trim the excess and half hitch the thread.

30. Wind the schlappen feather forward in even, open, controlled wraps, working toward the tying thread. Tease the fibers rearward after every turn so as not to trap any.

31. Remove a pair of barred Crazy Legs from a hank, and tie them in at the middle with two turns of thread. Position one on the near side of the hook and the other on the far side.

32. While maintaining tension on the thread, take two to three turns of thread over the center of the two Crazy Legs, then fold the rear sections rearward and return the thread to the base of the schlappen. Invert the hook in the vise.

33. Cut and clean a longer bundle of Arctic fox tail, comb out the underfur, and affix the bundle to the hook in the same manner as the rear section, reverse-tied.

34. Fold the fox rearward, and wind the thread over the bundle to form a bullet shape. After five or six tight wraps, half hitch the thread, and advance it in front of the bundle.

35. Flatten the head of the bundle with a pair of flat, non-serrated pliers. By doing so, you can affix the Helmet to the fly without issue, filling in the interior of the Helmet and preventing the Helmet from rolling.

36. Remove two small bundles of olive Laser Dub from a package and manipulate them in your hands to maximize length. Grab the two bundles by the middle with your tying hand, and transpose the bundles the front of the fly. Take two loose turns of thread around the middle of the bundles.

37. On the third turn of thread, pull tight on the thread, flaring the Laser Dub bundles in an X-shape while maintaining tension on the thread. The bundles should be on either side of the hook—not on the top or bottom.

38. While maintaining tension on the thread, advance it in front of the two Laser Dub bundles, teasing the bundles rearward.

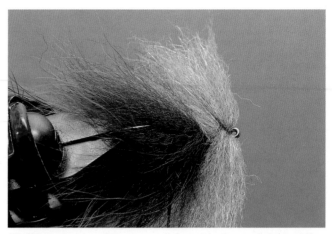

39. Wrap three or four turns of thread in front of the bundles, behind the hook eye. Half hitch the thread, then compete a four-turn whip-finish and trim the tying thread from the hook. Notice the Laser Dub is off to either side of the hook.

40. Place a small drop of gel Loctite Super Glue on the top and bottom of the hook, directly behind the eye, and slide your Sculpin Helmet over the eye of the hook. Notice the top or side with the eyes is actually facing the underside of the hook where the point is. This particular fly is tied in reverse to allow the fly to keel hook point up as a result of the Helmet.

41. Be sure to affix the Helmet far enough onto the hook so that the eye is exposed. Attach the tying thread behind the eye, and begin building a tapered thread head/dam behind the eye.

42. Continue winding thread behind the eye until you've built a neat, tapered thread head. Whip-finish, and trim the thread from the fly.

43. Complete the fly by adding a drop of epoxy or Clear Cure Goo Thin over the eyes for added durability, as well as cementing the thread wraps with Clear Cure Goo Hydro. If you have any space in between the thread head and the opening of the Sculpin Helmet, add some epoxy or Clear Cure Goo Thin to fill in the space.

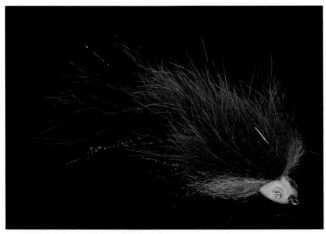

44. Notice how the finished fly lies flat with both hook points facing upward, which drastically reduces hang ups.

BROWN AND YELLOW HEADBANGER SCULPIN

Rear Hook:	#2 Gamakatsu SP11-3L3H or Partridge Universal Predator
Thread:	Dark brown 140-denier Ultra Thread
Tail:	Yellow Holographic Flashabou under 1 brown and 1 yellow marabou plume
Body:	Root beer Cactus Chenille (medium)
Hackle:	Yellow schlappen
Mottling:	Barred golden yellow/pearl flake Crazy Legs
Wing:	Brown Arctic fox tail
Connection:	Beadalon 19 Strand stringing wire (.018") with 2 Nuclear Corn Janns Netcraft ProEye 3D lure beads
Front Hook:	#1 Gamakatsu B10S or #2 Partridge Absolute Predator
Rear Collar:	Yellow Holographic Flashabou over 1 brown and 1 yellow marabou plume.
Body:	Root beer Cactus Chenille (medium)
Hackle:	Yellow schlappen
Mottling:	Barred golden yellow/pearl flake Crazy Legs
Wing:	Brown Arctic fox tail
Pectoral Fins:	Sculpin olive Senyo Laser Dub
Head:	Brown Fish-Skull Sculpin Helmet (large)

BROWN AND GINGER HEADBANGER SCULPIN

Rear Hook:	#2 Gamakatsu SP11-3L3H or Partridge Universal Predator
Thread:	Dark brown 140-denier Ultra Thread
Tail:	Copper Holographic Flashabou under 1 brown and 1 ginger marabou plume
Body:	Root beer Cactus Chenille (medium)
Hackle:	Fiery brown schlappen
Mottling:	Barred golden yellow/pearl flake Crazy Legs
Wing:	Chocolate brown Arctic fox tail
Connection:	Beadalon 19 Strand stringing wire (.018") with 2 Rusty Nail Janns Netcraft ProEye 3D lure beads
Front Hook:	#1 Gamakatsu B10S or #2 Partridge Absolute Predator
Rear Collar:	Copper Holographic Flashabou over 1 brown and 1 ginger marabou plume
Body:	Root beer Cactus Chenille (medium)
Hackle:	Fiery brown schlappen
Mottling:	Barred golden yellow/pearl flake Crazy Legs
Wing:	Chocolate brown Arctic fox tail
Pectoral Fins:	Sculpin olive Senyo Laser Dub
Head:	Brown Fish-Skull Sculpin Helmet (large)

FIERY BROWN AND GINGER HEADBANGER SCULPIN

Rear Hook:	#2 Gamakatsu SP11-3L3H or Partridge Universal Predator
Thread:	Rusty brown 140-denier Ultra Thread
Tail:	Brown Holographic Flashabou under 1 rusty brown and 1 ginger marabou plume
Body:	Root beer Cactus Chenille (medium)
Hackle:	Fiery brown schlappen
Mottling:	Barred golden yellow/pearl flake Crazy Legs
Wing:	Fiery brown Arctic fox tail
Connection:	Beadalon 19 Strand wire (.018") with 2 Rusty Nail Janns Netcraft ProEye 3D lure beads
Front Hook:	#1 Gamakatsu B10S or #2 Partridge Absolute Predator
Rear Collar:	Brown Holographic Flashabou over 1 rusty brown and 1 ginger marabou plume
Body:	Root beer Cactus Chenille (medium)
Hackle:	Fiery brown schlappen
Mottling:	Barred golden yellow/pearl flake Crazy Legs
Wing:	Fiery brown Arctic fox tail
Pectoral Fins:	Sculpin olive Senyo Laser Dub
Head:	Brown Fish-Skull Sculpin Helmet (large)

**TAN AND GINGER
HEADBANGER SCULPIN**

Rear Hook:	#2 Gamakatsu SP11-3L3H or Partridge Universal Predator
Thread:	Tan 140-denier Ultra Thread
Tail:	Gold Holographic Flashabou under 1 tan and 1 ginger marabou plume
Body:	Bonefish tan Cactus Chenille (medium)
Hackle:	Tan schlappen
Mottling:	Barred golden yellow/pearl flake Crazy Legs
Wing:	Light tan Arctic fox tail
Connection:	Beadalon 19 Strand stringing wire (.018") with 2 Cranberry Janns Netcraft ProEye 3D lure beads
Front Hook:	#1 Gamakatsu B10S or #2 Partridge Absolute Predator
Rear Collar:	Gold Holographic Flashabou over 1 tan and 1 ginger marabou plume
Body:	Bonefish Tan Cactus Chenille (medium)
Hackle:	Tan schlappen
Mottling:	Barred golden yellow/pearl flake Crazy Legs
Wing:	Light tan Arctic Fox Tail
Pectoral Fins:	Dark tan Senyo Laser Dub
Head:	Brown Fish-Skull Sculpin Helmet (large)

**BLACK
HEADBANGER SCULPIN**

Rear Hook:	#2 Gamakatsu SP11-3L3H or Partridge Universal Predator
Thread:	Black 140-denier Ultra Thread
Tail:	Red Holographic Flashabou under 2 black marabou plumes
Body:	Black Cactus Chenille (medium)
Hackle:	Black schlappen
Mottling:	Black/red flake Crazy Legs
Wing:	Black Arctic fox tail
Connection:	Beadalon 19 Strand stringing wire (.018") with 2 Cranberry Janns Netcraft ProEye 3D lure beads
Front Hook:	#1 Gamakatsu B10S or #2 Partridge Absolute Predator
Rear Collar:	Red Holographic Flashabou over two black marabou plumes
Body:	Black Cactus Chenille (medium)
Hackle:	Black schlappen
Mottling:	Black/red flake Crazy Legs
Wing:	Black Arctic fox tail
Pectoral Fins:	Black Senyo Laser Dub
Head:	Brown Fish-Skull Sculpin Helmet (large)

Index

Page numbers in italics indicate illustrations.